PURPOSE MINDSET

AKHTAR BADSHAH

PURPOSE MINDSET

HOW MICROSOFT INSPIRES EMPLOYEES & ALUMNI TO CHANGE THE WORLD

HarperCollins
LEADERSHIP

AN IMPRINT OF HarperCollins

Published by HarperCollins Leadership, an imprint of HarperCollins Focus LLC.

Book design by Aubrey Khan, Neuwirth & Associates

Any internet addresses, phone numbers, or company or product information printed in this book are offered as a resource and are not intended in any way to be or to imply an endorsement by HarperCollins Leadership, nor does Harper-Collins Leadership vouch for the existence, content, or services of these sites, phone numbers, companies, or products beyond the life of this book.

ISBN 978-1-4016-0369-4 (eBook)
ISBN 978-1-4016-0358-8 (HC)

Library of Congress Control Number: 2020943540

Printed in the United States of America
20 21 22 23 LSC 10 9 8 7 6 5 4 3 2 1

To Alka for setting the example for kindness and giving

"I cannot believe that the purpose of life is to be 'happy.' I think the purpose of life is to be useful, to be responsible, to be compassionate. It is, above all to matter: to count, to stand for something, to have made some difference that you lived at all."

—LEO ROSTEN (1908–1997),
humorist, screenwriter, political scientist

CONTENTS

Pillars of Purpose

by Brad Smith, President, Microsoft Corporation

I STILL REMEMBER ONE OF my first conversations with Akhtar Badshah. We had recruited Akhtar in 2004 to lead Microsoft's community affairs team, a precursor to what today we call Microsoft Philanthropies. It was a big job, as the team was already well on its way to becoming one of the largest corporate philanthropies in the world. We had hired Akhtar not only for the global perspective we thought he would bring to our work but for his personal passion and track record in delivering effective results in nonprofit work.

Over lunch in early 2005 in one of Microsoft's employee cafeterias, Akhtar and I debated the best way to build on the team that he'd inherited as the third leader of the company's philanthropic work in this field. It was already a broad foundation. Many people around the world are aware of the enormous financial success of Microsoft's founders and early employees, including Bill Gates. Less widely appreciated is the extraordinary degree to which Bill and his cofounder, Paul Allen, decided to distribute among employees so many shares in the company's stock, including through stock options. While this has evolved over the years, the broad distribution of stock remains a defining economic feature of Microsoft to this day.

As the world would witness, Microsoft changed the course of digital technology. This success created many affluent and even wealthy employees. The question was what all these individuals would do with their money. Many not surprisingly bought a larger home or a nicer car. But the good news was that a large majority of employees also thought about the world in broader terms. They increasingly asked what they could personally do to help make it better.

In no small measure, I have always attributed this to a second early decision by Microsoft's founding generation. They embraced a culture of giving that not only encouraged but celebrated volunteer and financial donations to local nonprofit groups. They created a "Giving Campaign" that matched employee cash contributions to nonprofits with an equal donation by Microsoft itself, initially up to $10,000 per year. (The amount today is $15,000.)

This early beginning sprung what is almost certainly the most generous employee donation program in the history of business. In recent months the total cumulative employee donations, including Microsoft's match, has topped $2 billion. The money has flowed literally to hundreds of thousands of nonprofits around the world. It has touched the lives of hundreds of millions of people.

As Akhtar and I discussed in 2005, when Microsoft approached what was that year its thirtieth birthday, this culture of giving created an opportunity to dream even bigger dreams. How could we contribute to more systemic, lasting, and positive change? How could we aim higher and become more strategic with Microsoft's philanthropic work? And how could this create new opportunities both for the institutions we would support and for the individuals who might get more involved?

In so many ways, this book highlights the answers that emerged. Told through the experiences of current and former Microsoft employees and nonprofit leaders around the world, *Purpose Mindset* lives up to its name. Reflecting years of thought borne from Akhtar's work and teaching, this book serves as a practical guide with lessons that are valuable for anyone who cares about helping to make the world a better place.

Along the way, Akhtar also has a knack for sharing a good story.

Many of these stories come from within Microsoft itself. These include Microsoft's "first couple," the label applied to Tricia and Jeff Raikes, who became the first Microsoft couple to get married. Since leaving the company, they have played an increasingly important and public role on issues like racial equity. Another is Jean-Philippe Courtois, one of Microsoft's most tenured executives. He has channeled the heartbreak of losing a son into a family foundation that is making a difference for a new generation of young entrepreneurs around the world.

Other lessons come from work done elsewhere, including by Microsoft alumni. One of my favorites is about Paul Maritz, who became the CEO of VMware in 2008 and injected into his new company the culture of giving that he had experienced at Microsoft. Paul's ultimate lesson speaks to anyone wanting to drive this type of cultural change. As he recounts, he came to appreciate the lesson he shared with his new employees. Philanthropy is not only about contributing to other people's lives. It is also about transforming your own.

The work is not easy, and it requires determination and a long-term commitment. It is illustrated well in the experience of Trish Millines Dziko, an African American woman whom Akhtar rightly describes as a "Seattle institution." She has brought access to technology to a new generation of underrepresented and underserved communities, learning from experience what it takes to make philanthropic work successful.

Importantly, *Purpose Mindset* also shares lessons from mistakes easily made even by well-intentioned individuals who embrace volunteer and philanthropic opportunities. One of my favorites comes in Chapter Four, as Akhtar writes about how easy it is for individuals who have been successful in one part of their life to become "cocky and arrogant" as they engage in something new and different. It's an important insight for all of us. And it helps explain why a purpose mindset needs to build on a growth mindset—an approach that starts with a recognition that we all have far more to learn that we may even recognize.

All this has become more important and urgent with the dawn of a new decade. The year 2020 brought first a pandemic that is unprecedented in our lifetimes. It has been followed by a national reawakening across the United States regarding the systemic racism that has persisted in our country for more than four centuries. At Microsoft, both issues have called on us to assess anew how we can contribute more purposefully and positively to better meet the nation's needs—not just for some people but for everyone. We have taken new steps, recognizing that they are just the first of many new steps we and others will need to take together.

Ultimately, *Purpose Mindset* speaks powerfully to one of the great questions of our time: how can we each find more purpose in our work and lives? We each can develop "pillars of purpose" that make our days more rewarding. In the world of work, this hopefully begins with the sense of purpose we find in our day jobs, including the products we work on and the customers we serve. It extends to the meaning we find in our connections with colleagues and friends. Ultimately, it extends to the opportunity we each have to contribute to a better world in the broadest possible sense, including the causes we share and the time we commit to advance them.

Whether it's a new chapter in life or just an added step for tomorrow, *Purpose Mindset* provides insightful and inspiring opportunities to learn from the experiences of others—and an author who has devoted a career to applying them himself.

ACKNOWLEDGMENTS

THIS BOOK, OR AT LEAST the idea for this book, had been in the making for many years, from the time I was at Microsoft. When I left Microsoft, I started thinking more about it, developed an outline, and conducted a few interviews. But nothing came out of it because I just did not move forward with it. There was always something else pressing that needed to get done. I was teaching several new classes, starting a consulting practice, and introducing a new leadership development program called Accelerating Social Transformation (AST), which I offer through the University of Washington's Evans School of Public Policy & Governance.

In late 2018, I shared the idea for the book with Ali Spain, the executive director of the Microsoft Alumni Network. She loved the idea and immediately sent the outline to a former colleague of hers at Microsoft, Jeff James, who was now the publisher at HarperCollins Leadership. A few months later, I got a note stating that they were very interested in publishing the book and asking if I could have it completed by early October 2019. I had not written a single word besides the outline. The credit for getting me on the path of writing goes to Ali, without whose initial push and introductions at HarperCollins Leadership, this book would still be in my head.

My editor, Tim Burgard, was very supportive in getting me started and was flexible enough to extend my deadline to the end of February 2020. For me, writing does not come easy. I am very good at public speaking and am a very visual person. To write meant that I had to redevelop the muscles and discipline to interview, transcribe, absorb, and then write as much as possible as my schedule allowed. To get the writing done, I got help from numerous individuals along the way. A casual conversation with my friend and colleague Nalini Iyer, who teaches at Seattle University, led to me meeting Rose Ernst, who is an academic editor and consultant. I was not writing an academic book, but Iyer urged me to chat with her. Ernst is a brilliant editor but most importantly a great listener and someone who took many of my complex ideas and turned them into a structure that made sense. It was her effective editing that also kept me on track to finish the book.

When I started writing, I wanted to cover lots of different ideas. But while many were important, they were not necessarily central to the theme and the story that needed to be told. My two friends Shiv Bakhshi and Arun Jain were instrumental in helping me sort through many of these ideas and developing a cogent narrative. Genevieve Trembley, a colleague at my consulting firm, Catalytic Innovators Group, spent countless hours with me working through the ideas of the purpose mindset that we have used in multiple trainings and presentations over the last year. It has been fun bouncing ideas off of her.

Laura Vergara, a former student of mine at the Evans School, worked with me to develop the principles of the purpose mindset very early on last summer. It was while we worked together on AST that she helped me to focus the path I would take in writing this book. She has always emphasized that my writings should look at things through a social justice and equity lens. Her friendly criticisms have allowed me to sharpen my ideas, and her constant input has been instrumental in developing the five principles of the purpose mindset.

Julia Nussenbaum, also a student of mine at the Evans School, has helped me with several drafts, sourcing the material I needed to clearly articulate my ideas.

I was fortunate to have many highly accomplished individuals give me their time for the book, inviting me into their lives and sharing with me their journey and life experiences. I will cherish these conversations. Each one has highlighted the deep roots of humanity every one of us has. I am grateful that I was able to highlight their work and how they are changing the world. Their work has been the inspiration for this book, and I hope it inspires many of you to become purposeful in your lives and contribute to making a positive difference. I have hoped to capture their work in the spirit it was recounted to me, and any mistakes and omissions are mine alone. There are thousands of Microsoft employees and alumni doing amazing work to change the world. There are many others whom I should have profiled, but in the end I had to choose to share a sample of stories that were both diverse and reflective of the amazing work being done. Again, these choices are mine alone. I hope that this book becomes a catalyst for more such stories to be told.

I want to thank Bill Gates, Satya Nadella, Brad Smith (who was also kind enough to write the foreword), and William Neukom for spending time with me and sharing their insights and wisdom. My former boss Pamela Passman—we had a good time reminiscing about some of the steps we undertook in 2004–05 to revitalize the employee giving campaign and continue to add fuel to the giving machine. Mary Snapp, Kate Behncken—both took on the leadership after me for providing the new contexts and how the giving program has continued to evolve, mature, and grow; and Karen Bergin who is leading the Microsoft employee giving program.

I also want to thank my friends and colleagues: Carol Cone, Aaron Hurst, Chris Jarvis, Jens Molbak, Susan McPherson, and Raj Sisodia for their insights and contributions. My friend Samir Bodas for sharing the work his company is doing to support the community during the Covid-19 crisis. There are many other friends and colleagues who have provided insights and encouragement over supper, a glass of wine, or through casual conversations. It is these short conversations that helped bring multiple ideas together and helped me piece a narrative that I have described. My immense gratitude to all of them.

My kids—Anish, Aseem, and Akash—are all part of the generation that has embodied a sense of purpose, which they bring to their lives and work every day. They have become smart, caring, mature, and knowledgeable adults, and our regular conversations have contributed many of the ideas I have shared here.

Finally, my wife, Alka, has been with me throughout this journey. I would have never been introduced to Microsoft's employee giving campaign had she not joined Microsoft and moved to Seattle in 1998, where I was able to experience the spirit of this campaign as a spouse. This experience was what first got me thinking about the unique generosity emanating from one company. She is a quiet force, gently pushing me to write, patiently listening to my ramblings, and gently helping me find the most salient ideas that should be put on paper. She has been the constant strength that has helped drive and support the sense of purpose that I have been able to live and write about. For that, I am eternally grateful.

Purpose is that renewable source of energy that continues to drive humanity forward; without purpose we lose our path. This book is meant to inspire all of us especially in these very challenging times to discover purpose, build on it, and keep that eternal flame going.

IN 2001, A GIANT EARTHQUAKE hit the state of Gujarat in India. The devastation was shocking in scale and hit me personally. I had previously lived in Ahmedabad, the largest city in Gujarat, for six years as a student and still had many friends there. Ahmedabad was hundreds of miles from the quake's epicenter, but several buildings collapsed there because of the intensity of the quake. In all, twenty thousand people died, more than 150,000 were injured, and millions of lives were impacted by the physical damage. I visited the town of Bhuj in March 2001, a few months after the earthquake. Bhuj was at the epicenter, and I was shocked to see the scale of the destruction: every building was destroyed.

At that time, the Indian community in the Seattle area was small but influential, and several of us quickly mobilized to provide relief and support back home. Many other concentrations of the Indian diaspora also mobilized, like in the Bay Area. In Seattle itself, we raised close to $1 million. The speed and size of the generosity made me appreciate the ability of small organizations to mobilize quickly and provide a prompt response. We mobilized hundreds of people in the Puget Sound area to contribute to this cause.

Major contributions came from Microsoft employees and its alumni, and I was touched to see the generosity of people that none of us knew. My twelve-year-old son created a toy drive at his middle school with some friends, and they raised more than $700. My eldest son's school custodian gave him $100, a significant amount given his weekly salary. An elderly woman came to our offices and handed me a five-dollar bill. She was sad she could not do more. I was stunned. Why were so many folks showing up to be a part of something so far away?

Was this unique to Seattle? Or was there something more to it? I asked this question because in 1993 I joined the Mega Cities Project, a nonprofit focused on sharing what worked in large cities, those with more than ten million inhabitants. During that period, I started investigating the role of corporations in the well-being of cities. Organizations such as London First, New York City Partnership, and The Atlanta Project (TAP) were bringing city, business, and community leaders together to work to improve civic life. In that process, I had observed how companies and their employees could together contribute to the well-being of their communities.

Bill Gates shared with me that in cities like Seattle or Cincinnati, which are not too big, some of the top business leaders and other community leaders did mobilize around civic issues, such as the convention center or the clean water efforts; but other efforts led by Paul Allen around the Parks Initiative failed.

During this current coronavirus crisis, Challenge Seattle, which was launched as an alliance of nineteen of the region's largest employers in 2015 under the leadership of former governor Christine Gregoire, has developed an unprecedented partnership with the public sector to flatten the curve and has become the role model for other cities.[1] This could be why I experienced this outpouring of support from the Seattle community during the Gujarat Earthquake: there is this network of community and business leaders that care, and this caring extends to everyone, including those who are new to the community.

Another key organization is the United Way of King County, which has played a central role in urging corporate employees to contribute and become engaged in civic efforts to improve cities. They have a day of caring, in which corporate volunteers go out into their city and work on various projects, such as painting classrooms, cleaning up the environment, and so on.

The Great Machine—
Microsoft's Employee Giving Program

I first observed Microsoft's employee giving campaigns in 1993, shortly after my wife, Alka, joined Microsoft on the East Coast. I was fascinated by how Microsoft employees were so motivated to join other employees and participate in supporting causes. Many took on issues they cared about individually, but others joined at the request of their friends and colleagues. Why do some people support efforts that they might have no personal connection to?

When we moved to Seattle in 1998, I connected with Microsoft employees and alumni through my nonprofit, Digital Partners Foundation, and was struck once again by how active Microsoft employees were in their community, giving their time and resources to causes both close to home and afar. Though corporate matching gifts and philanthropy programs are not unique to Microsoft, what is unique is how Microsoft has organized its employee giving as a campaign. Every October, employees can mobilize for a cause they wish to support and solicit other employees to join them. This institutional structure has shaped the culture of the company and shaped the behavior of its employees and alumni, an interesting phenomenon I wanted to explore and write about.

Bill Gates also shared with me how his parents played a central role in shaping his values. He grew up in a household where his parents were always serving in the community. "My parents were always good about talking about the things they were doing in the community. I was always involved in the school levy efforts; my parents had me hold signs, even though I did not go to a public school. I would have benefited from that," says Gates. Mary Gates served on the national board of the United Way; Bill Gates Sr. served on the boards of Planned Parenthood and the Municipal League, among many other charitable causes. In 1983, at the urging of his mother, Mary Gates, Bill Gates had Microsoft launch an employee payroll deduction effort to support the United Way of King County. This effort raised $17,000 that first year and, as of this writing, it is set to cross the $2 billion mark. I have been fascinated by how this modest beginning has grown from a *moment* to a *movement* that has impacted millions of lives. In the Seattle community, Microsoft employees' and alumni's generosity are well known, and it would be difficult to find a nonprofit that has not benefited in some way from this generosity. Microsoft's contribution to improving the lives of millions of people around the world through its support of philanthropic efforts, however, is a story that is not as well known.

This book is anchored in my personal and professional experiences from my time at Microsoft, where I led its philanthropic efforts for ten years and oversaw the employee giving program. In this role, I observed the impact that Microsoft, its employees, and its alumni had on communities around the world. My goal is to capture the story behind this movement through the eyes of key participants, especially alumni and current Microsoft leaders.

I also explore why certain people are driven by purpose to move beyond personal growth to making an impact on society. I hope readers will see how they, too, can move from a growth mindset to a purpose mindset and ignite their own movements to create positive change. I also hope that other companies can glean lessons from Microsoft's efforts and be inspired to create their own institutional structures that enable a culture of purpose and empathy.

Today's employees increasingly look at a company's mission before joining it. Prospective employees tend to focus not only on opportunities for professional growth but also on how they can contribute to something greater than themselves. The Edelman Trust Barometer, a global online survey taken every year, consistently shows that there's not much trust in business. But the 2019 results showed a bright spot: "Employees are ready and willing to trust their employers, but the trust must be earned through more than 'business as usual.' Employees' expectations that prospective employers will join them in taking action on societal issues (67 percent) is nearly as high as their expectations of personal empowerment (74 percent)."[2]

Movement to Movements

Corporate employee-matching gift programs and corporate philanthropy are not new, and for decades corporations have invested in these kinds of efforts. It is hard to pin down the exact date when corporate social responsibility began, but some attribute it to Adam Smith, "the father of capitalism," who in his treatise *The Wealth of Nations* argued that market forces driven by individuals and corporations should serve and advance the needs of society. On the other side of the argument has been Milton Friedman, a prominent economist and Nobel Prize winner, who stated that business simply had one responsibility: increase profits for shareholders.

In 2019, the Business Roundtable announced a new Statement on the Purpose of a Corporation signed by 181 CEOs who committed to lead their companies for the benefit of all stakeholders—customers, employees, suppliers, communities, and shareholders. This is a massive shift in the role of business: "Since 1978, Business Roundtable has periodically issued Principles of Corporate Governance. Each version of the document issued since 1997 has endorsed principles of shareholder primacy—that corporations exist principally to serve shareholders. With today's announcement, the new Statement supersedes previous statements and outlines a modern standard for corporate responsibility."[3]

Archie B. Carrol provides an excellent summary of the evolution and impact of corporate social responsibility (CSR) in his article "A History of Corporate Social Responsibility: Concepts and Practices."[4] There are others who have questioned how sincere companies are in their practice of CSR, seeing it as "green washing." Others have seen CSR, or corporate philanthropy, as just a way to pay a tax to continue doing business as usual. In *Winners Take All*, Anand Giridharadas has questioned global elites' efforts to change the world, wondering whether companies shouldn't first do more to change their practices in the products they make and sell and in how they pay and provide benefits to their employees.

Microsoft also has a CSR program and philanthropic efforts, but what stands out to me is the depth of its employee giving and matching gift programs. Microsoft is not unique in this. The first corporate employee matching gift program was launched in 1954 by General Electric, and since then major corporations have developed programs to encourage their employees to volunteer and invest in the community.[5]

What is unique, however, is the structure that was developed to nurture a fledgling program that started in 1983 and help it grow into the culture of the entire company, a culture that continues to thrive outside of the company in its alumni. I had a front-row seat to see how the institutional structure has supported its employees over four decades, giving individuals the opportunity to focus on the common good.

Microsoft was born in the information technology age and has seen amazing growth. Its stock price rose very rapidly in the 1990s, creating an estimated twelve thousand millionaires among its employees. Given this wealth, it may seem obvious that employees had become comfortable enough to contribute to outside causes. But what is interesting is that during my time at Microsoft the stock was mostly flat and there was a recession, yet the employee generosity continued to grow.

What is the secret sauce of this unprecedented level of employee generosity and how has this translated into so many Microsoft alumni turning philanthropy into a way of life? Leslie Lenkowsky, a professor of public affairs and philanthropy at Indiana University, has pointed out that "some Silicon Valley folks are operating off a different model, not necessarily using their companies for philanthropy but rather using their own wealth." This is true of the leadership at Microsoft, where Bill Gates, Paul Allen, Steve Ballmer, and other senior Microsoft executives have started their own foundations and become leaders in philanthropy. From my interviews with Microsoft alumni, I discovered they all have one aspect in common—they were all inspired by Microsoft leaders getting intimately involved and actively participating in the employee giving program.

Bill Gates is proud of how the company leadership was actively involved and how the employee giving campaign became part of the company culture. "Steve Ballmer came from Procter & Gamble where they sort of forced everybody to give their fair share, and so his initial attitude was, 'Do we want to impose this on people?' But he eventually got enthused about making this a thing where we would come together." The employee giving program was that initial exposure that eventually shaped many of the Microsoft leaders to launch their own philanthropic organizations and has cumulatively spurred a rethinking of what effective philanthropy and positive social change consists of. These leaders have inspired many Microsoft employees and newer tech titans on how to effectively deploy their wealth for societal change. In the COVID-19 crisis, many of these same individuals have stepped up with their philanthropic giving with more than $30 million being pledged through All in Seattle, another $23 million being pledged to the Seattle Foundation, and individual contributions going to the University of Washington toward the coronavirus response with a $10 million contribution from the Ballmer Foundation. The Bill and Melinda Gates Foundation has committed $355 million so far for the pandemic response.

Bill Gates and Paul Allen founded Microsoft in 1975. Their goal was a computer on every desk and in every home. Over the last forty-five years, Microsoft and its products have changed the way we use information technology, how we work, communicate, and entertain ourselves. Today, Microsoft is one of the world's largest software makers[6] and one of the world's most valuable companies by market capitalization.[7] The untold story is how Microsoft also inspired its employees to not only create change through their work but also in their communities.

I explore how Microsoft created a culture of empathy and purpose that continues to live outside of its corporate offices and has spawned thousands of change agents around the world. How has a modest employee giving and payroll deduction effort in 1983 morphed into one of the world's largest employee-driven giving campaigns?

The Changemakers

When I joined Digital Partners Foundation in early 2000, I kept running into Microsoft alumni who had left the company to launch social organizations that went on to improve the lives of poor people at a massive scale. I was curious about why these folks quit their jobs to start a nonprofit. People like:

- John Wood, who started Room to Read. On a trek to Nepal in 1999, he was amazed by the warmth and enthusiasm of students and teachers he met but saddened by the shocking lack of resources. He quit his position at Microsoft and launched Room to Read, which today has more than 35,000 schools/libraries and has benefited 16.8 million children.

- Patrick Awuah, who in 1997 left Microsoft to start Ashesi University in his home country, Ghana. The mission of Ashesi University is to educate ethical, entrepreneurial leaders in Africa; to cultivate the critical thinking skills, the concern for others, and the courage it will take to transform the continent.[8] What makes a software engineer quit his job to create a university that is now ranked among the top in Africa?

- Trish Millines Dzkio, who left Microsoft in 1996 to launch Technology Access Foundation. TAF is now a leader in providing a STEM (science, technology, engineering, and math) education to underserved students in the public school system. She also led TAF in creating the only public school, TAF Academy, in Washington State that is comanaged by a nonprofit and a school district.

- Paul Shoemaker, who left Microsoft in 1998 to become the founding president of Social Venture Partners. During his time at SVP, he created a global movement to get technology experts and other professionals to come together to invest in social change. SVP now operates in more than forty countries.

After joining Microsoft, I continued to meet more folks all over the world who had left Microsoft to focus on new endeavors focused on driving societal change. Tazin Shadid left Microsoft in 2011 to start Spreeha with a hope of empowering underprivileged people in Bangladesh break the cycle of poverty. Shadid joined Microsoft as a software engineer in 2005, and while working there, he volunteered to run a health care program for people living in the urban slums of Dhaka, Bangladesh.

Though shares declined as Microsoft grew in the 2000s, employee generosity did not wane. I had a front-row seat when I joined the company in 2004 to lead its philanthropic efforts. I interacted with many employees who became deeply engaged in launching social impact initiatives while they worked at Microsoft, and I met alumni who left the company to launch organizations and became leaders in their new field, fueling innovation for social change.

I came to understand the employee giving campaign and how Bill Gates and Paul Allen, in creating their foundations, inspired others to also invest their time, talent, and treasure for societal transformation.

Unlike Bill Gates and Paul Allen, the individuals featured here were not billionaires who could quit their jobs without worrying about ever working again. Some continued to work at Microsoft while focusing on social sector work in their free time. Some took great financial risks by quitting their tech jobs to move to the nonprofit sector or start their own organizations, and many faced periods of financial instability and doubt during the process. Continuing to work in high-paying tech jobs probably would have been the "reasonable" choice for most of these people. But they all decided to be "unreasonable" and ventured out to make a change. They were all committed to the idea of using their positions of power to help empower others. As Trish Millines Dzkio says, "You have it, you share it."

What is common to each story is that all these individuals were driven to seize their moment. You will learn how they started their initiatives and the role Microsoft and the employee giving campaign played in inspiring them to use their talent and resources to create societal change. I share lessons from this culture of giving that over time has become part of the DNA of the company.

My hope is to inspire readers to seize moments and turn them into movements for social change. The book will also provide a better understanding of how company culture can drive employees to believe in a purpose and create a culture of empathy.

Getting to the Purpose Mindset

In *The Purpose Effect*, Dan Pontefract describes the connections between the three crucial areas of purpose: personal, organizational, and workplace. He argues that if there is an interconnection between the three distinct definitions of purpose, then the benefits will accrue to every stakeholder from employees to society. Raj Sisodia, the coauthor of *Conscious Capitalism* and *The Healing Organization,* in my interview with him described purpose "as the kind of fuel that brings the next tier of energy and capacity in people."

Purpose, and the commitment to create purpose, is becoming critical as we are increasingly driven by the growth mindset based on the seminal work done by Carol S. Dweck in her book *Mindset: The New Psychology of Success.* While Dweck focuses on unleashing one's passion, growing as an individual, taking on more challenges, learning new things, and reaching higher levels of achievement and ability, the purpose mindset builds on the growth mindset and extends the benefits beyond the self for the greater good, as former labor secretary Robert Reich calls for in his book *The Common Good.* It is about rediscovering and unleashing the common good. (See Figure 1.)

FIXED MINDSET	GROWTH MINDSET	PURPOSE MINDSET
Seek perfection and avoid failure	Learners who seek growth and development	Focus on the common good
Focus on reproducing what they know	Focus on improving what and how they do	Inspiring action by being constructively actionable
Focus on perfecting their abilities—not learning new skills	Believes strengths can be developed with effort, reaching higher levels of achievement and ability	Believes in developing their strengths and contributing to the future of greater possibilities

Adapted from Benefit Mindset: Good Business Guide @ benefitmindset.com

FIGURE 1

Aaron Hurst in his book *The Purpose Economy* maps people into three categories: people who are driven by purpose, people driven by wealth, and people driven by status. In this research, he also found that purpose-oriented people are 64 percent more likely to be fulfilled than their colleagues who see work as being about financial gain or status. He also goes on to say, "Being a Purpose-Oriented Worker is also not about the industry you are in or a job you have. Contrary to what we might assume, Purpose-Oriented Workers are not all teachers and social workers. They are accountants, lawyers, assistants, salespeople, and janitors."[9] I have followed Hurst's book in my classroom and also in the training I conduct through Accelerating Social Transformation. I had early conversations with Hurst about my book and its focus. Hurst coined 'purpose mindset' and encouraged me to use it as the title of my book, for which I am very grateful. By highlighting what constitutes a purpose mindset, I hope to inspire the reader how to activate purpose in everything they do.

In *The Second Mountain: The Quest for a Moral Life*, David Brooks responds to what he frames as the "six decades [of] the worship of the self [that] has been a central preoccupation of our culture—molding the self, investing in the self, expressing the self. Capitalism, the meritocracy, and the modern social science have normalized selfishness; they have made it seem that the only human motives that are real are the self-interested ones—the desire for money, status and power. They silently spread the message that giving, care and love are just icing on the cake of society."[10] My own experience and my work show that people are not just driven by a growth mindset; rather, many of them use the growth mindset to make the world a better place: they care for the common good, and in doing so extend into the purpose mindset.

Satya Nadella became the third CEO of Microsoft in February 2014. Since then he has transformed the culture of the company from being hypercompetitive to also including a sense of purpose and empathy, especially how the company operates and how employees show up for work. "Culture is what allows you to live your sense of purpose and mission, and this has been very helpful in both staying focused on what is uniquely Microsoft to contribute, and then finding inspiration in our culture to do more," says Nadella.

Kathleen Hogan, the chief people officer at Microsoft, has been charged with implementing this changing culture of purpose and empathy. In her interview with Catherina Bulgarella for *Forbes*, Hogan outlines the five Ps as: pay, perks, people, pride, and purpose. This became a cohesive road map to support Microsoft's transformation, almost organically, from an organization of know-it-alls into an organization of learn-it-alls.[11]

In the chapters that follow, I outline what it takes to develop purpose and highlight five principles of the purpose mindset that, in addition to the growth mindset, can help an organization fulfill its promise to society to benefit the common good. These principles are also a source to reignite our personal energy. The Five Principles that drive an individual to develop a purpose mindset are:

1.   **Discovering Strengths**—working from strengths and building on them to create greater possibilities.
2.   **Working from Abundance**—accessing a variety of innovative resources, from people to equipment and space, at previously unthinkable scales.
3.   **Extending the Common Good**—moving from doing things efficiently to having an impact on broad community progress.
4.   **Igniting Movements**—focusing on building a movement, not an organization, that leads to societal change.
5.   **Embracing Empathy and Compassion**—centering on the "we" rather than the "me."

Microsoft president Brad Smith summed it best when he said to me, "You know we want to encourage people to adopt a learn-it-all attitude in everything they do, from the most exciting to the most mundane. I do think that most people in life find it easier to get excited and learn more when they're doing things that they are passionate about. And so, I think that a purpose-driven mindset and mission-driven orientation tends to influence everything we do. In effect, it imbues itself in every corner of the company."

Today, as humanity is coming to grips with the COVID-19 pandemic, which has spread to all corners of the world with many parts of the economy coming to a standstill, we are seeing new rays of hope: individuals, communities, and businesses working together to find creative and innovative solutions to overcome this crisis. The only way we are going to continue to strive for our humanity is to move from the "me" to the "we" attitude, and the purpose mindset will be critical. As the great Albus Percival Wulfric Brian Dumbledore says in the movie *Harry Potter and the Prisoner of Azkaban*: "Happiness can be found, even in the darkest of times, if one only remembers to turn on the light."

My hope is that the stories of changemakers that follow inspire readers to see how each one of us can turn on the light, through small or big acts of purposeful interventions, and bend the arc of humanity and create a better world for all. As Martin Luther King Jr. said in one of his powerful speeches, "The arc of the moral universe is long, but it bends towards justice."[12]

PURPOSE
MINDSET

CHAPTER ONE

The Great Giving Machine

Entrepreneurs have a singular focus—create a great company and make sure the company survives, thrives, and grows. Philanthropy and giving back to the community are not necessarily a priority when the company is young and still on its growth trajectory—especially not in the 1980s. That's why it's important to delve into how Microsoft launched an employee giving campaign that has continued to grow itself and its impact around the world. This book and this chapter focus on how a young technology company established its employee giving and corporate philanthropy program in the early- to mid-1980s, which has subsequently grown into this "great giving machine" over the past thirty-five years.

On a cold December morning in 2017, I interviewed Bill Neukom at the Four Seasons Hotel in Seattle for his insights on how and why Microsoft decided to invest in the community and launch the employee giving and matching program. As the head of Microsoft's philanthropy program from 2004 to 2014, I had a good sense of the program and its impact in the community, in Seattle and around the world. I was curious, however, about the program's genesis.

This genesis can be traced to Neukom's journey to becoming Microsoft's chief legal officer. He was born into a comfortable middle-class family; his father led the West Coast and Asia practice for a leading business consulting firm. Though his father led a busy life, he served the community and chaired the United Way of California board for several years. Neukom's mother was active with Planned Parenthood and other local advocacy organizations that worked on social justice issues. According to Neukom, "It was their intellectual curiosity and agility that caused them to think more broadly and invest time in the community."

Neukom graduated from Stanford Law School and then clerked for the King County superior court in Seattle between 1967 and 1968. He then joined MacDonald Hoague & Bayless, an unconventional law firm focusing on civil rights and immigration law. The firm represented many minority organizations, such as the Urban League and the Neighborhood House. "My workplace became [a] sort of a laboratory for involvement in the community because we were very much the community's lawyers," he says. "We did not have many business clients, certainly no public companies, and it wasn't that we wouldn't have been happy to do that. But our clientele were largely individuals, community organizations, and small businesses."

Neukom's relationship with Bill Gates Sr. began through bar association activities. Bill Gates Sr. was the head of the King County Bar Association, and Neukom was the head of the young lawyers in King County. During the '60s and '70s, with the backdrops of the Civil Rights Movement and the Vietnam War, many younger lawyers felt newfound responsibility to become politically active and to give back to their communities.

A seminal moment for Neukom was when Bill Gates Sr. stood up to the opposition from established members of the bar association to start a law school scholarship for minorities. According to Neukom, "This must have been [the] early '80s, late '70s. There was no such scholarship out there, and it was something like $5,000 or $10,000. We had the money from dues, and the board exercising its fiduciary duty decided this would be a good use of that money. Some people didn't like it. Some members called

[for] a special meeting of the King County Bar [to] be convened at the Washington Athletic Club. With his image and his law firm's reputation at stake, he stood tall in front of the members and faced them down. We prevailed in a vote, and to this day the King County Bar is continuing to invest its membership dues in this scholarship. Talk about a profile in courage." He continues, "So I came to Microsoft with the belief that the company could do some good. Part of it was because of seeing law firms do good, part was my family exposure, and part of it was just that the more I looked around, the more it seemed to me that businesses could be agents of reform in a positive way."

Still part of Shidler, McBroom, Gates, and Lucas (Bill Gates Sr.'s firm), Neukom did legal work for Microsoft when the company had just twelve employees. He joined Microsoft as its first general counsel in 1985 and was with the company until 2002. He was instrumental in developing the ethos of giving at Microsoft from its early days and instituting the culture that turned giving into a way of life.

The Moment—for the Great Giving Machine

In his book *Showing Up for Life*, Bill Gates Sr. eloquently describes his ethos: "I show up because I care about a cause. Or because I care about the person who asked me to show up. And maybe sometimes I show up because it irritates me when other people *don't* show up."[1] When Bill Neukom showed up at Microsoft in 1985, he made two critical decisions that have since impacted millions of lives over the last thirty-five years and have been instrumental in creating a program that has inspired thousands of employees to become engaged deeply into their communities. The first was the creation of the Community Affairs Department as part of the legal group that would focus on the company's philanthropic efforts, and second was the introduction of the employee giving charitable match for every full-time employee in the United States. These two decisions were the *moment* that enabled many Microsoft employees to not only activate their generosity but become inspired to create their own *movements* as changemakers.

Neukom persuaded Bill Gates and Jon Shirley (then president of Microsoft) that the legal department should also include three other disciplines—Government Affairs, Industry Affairs, and Community Affairs. Neukom thought Community Affairs was important because he was convinced the business community could play an important role in advancing community causes and that Microsoft should be a part of that.

In 1985, when Neukom joined the company, the workforce was very young. They worked extremely long hours fulfilling the company's mission of a computer on every desk and every home. They did not have the time to focus on anything else. The challenge was to involve this young workforce to care about the community. For Neukom, this was a perfect opportunity, creating an employee giving program that was both fun and educational. Over time, as the employees matured and established roots in the community, the program also grew and matured.

Community Affairs has two major responsibilities: guiding the company's direct investment into the community and guiding an employee program to encourage philanthropy. On the employee philanthropy front, the first employee giving effort was launched in 1983 with the United Way at the urging of Bill Gates's mother, Mary Gates, who was deeply involved with the local and national United Way. She encouraged her son to start an employee payroll-deduction effort so that employees could donate to the United Way and have their donation get deducted bimonthly from their paychecks. With an initial thousand-dollar match, this effort raised $17,000. According to Brad Smith, Microsoft's president and chief legal officer, "I think that in the early years it was perceived in part as simply an employee benefit. And you know this was at a time when companies were not trying to provide free food for everybody in cafeterias and free laundry service and other things that they could generally afford themselves. A free matching gift was something that people might value, and sure enough they did."

After Neukom established the giving effort within Community Affairs, he convinced Bill Gates and John Shirley to increase the match to $10,000; in 1990, the match was expanded to any registered nonprofit of the employee's choice. It is an astounding figure for 1985 and would lead to amazing results. Microsoft's evolving employee giving program has generated over $1.8 billion in total, affected tens of thousands of nonprofits every year, and redefined how purpose and empathy can be harmonized with careers and the instinct to do good for the community. Gates felt that it was important to set a high ceiling to encourage giving. He was somewhat disappointed that in the early years "people did take advantage of the match but not as much as I thought they would." The match was the key where you could double your money to the community. "In the early days, employees were donating to their alma mater, and then eventually certain environmental causes caught on as well and some local causes including Planned Parenthood that did pretty well," he says. In the early nineties, Gates had this realization: "Well, should I really build the company for all this giving?" Fortunately, the employee giving program had established deep enough roots and had become part of the company culture, and the program continued to grow and extend that benefit to thousands of nonprofits.

For Gates, United Way King County was central to the employee giving campaign. With his family's rich history with it, he felt United Way opened up opportunities for employees to get connected to their communities and get a better perspective of the needs. "In a technology company, you are hiring people from a global marketplace, and many come from outside the United States," he says. "These employees have had no exposure to charitable giving, and even if they come from other parts of the US, they don't know the agencies in Seattle, they have not been to a food bank or homeless shelter, so it is an unnatural match." United Way served a purpose to connect the dots for the employees.

Corporate Matching Gift Programs

Corporate philanthropy has a long history in the United States. Since the seventeenth century, business leaders have donated to social causes. Such gifts were made by individuals, however, as there were legal restrictions that prevented companies from meddling in social affairs. It was only in the mid-1950s, after a series of legal decisions, that the last of these barriers fell, and companies started to develop employee giving and corporate giving programs.[2] General Electric established the first corporate employee matching gift program in 1954. Since that point, GE has matched over $1.07 billion in donations to nonprofits. Last year alone, the GE match was $39 million. In the Tech Sector, Apple introduced its $10,000 per year employee match in 2011 when Tim Cook became CEO. Apple raised more than $50 million in 2014 when it expanded the program to all the countries in which it has a presence. In 2018, Apple's employee giving program topped $125 million.[3] These programs are not limited to the tech sector. Pepsi offers to match gifts up to $10,000 per year per employee, and it matches at a 2:1 ratio if the employee volunteers more than fifty hours with a single organization. Johnson & Johnson matches up to $20,000 per year at a 2:1 ratio for full-time employees and at 1:1 for part-time employees and retirees. Soros Fund Management has one of the most generous programs, matching donations of up to $100,000 at a 3:1 ratio. Some companies have more creative matching programs. For example, Nestle gives employees two extra days of personal time off if they donate a full day's pay to a nonprofit, and the company will also match that donation. While many companies offer generous matching programs, other large companies like Amazon and Facebook were late to launch their employee matching programs.[4]

Priming the Giving Machine

By the time I joined Microsoft in 2004 to head Community Affairs, four additional important decisions had been made that would further fuel the "great giving machine." In 2002, Pamela Passman was appointed as the corporate vice president for corporate affairs in the law and corporate affairs group. She made three decisions. First, she convinced then CEO Steve Ballmer that the employee giving budget should be budgeted as an employee benefit within human resources rather than part of the philanthropic budget. She argued that as the employee base grew and the popularity of the employee giving campaign grew, the philanthropic budget was under constant pressure. Making the giving program an HR benefit would free up Community Affairs funds for ongoing community-based projects. More importantly, by moving the budget within HR it would ensure its permanency and be treated similarly to other employee benefits. According to Passman, "This was the fastest decision that I had seen Steve make. It showed that, at the highest level, leadership was committed to support employees to follow their passions."

The second decision, also in 2002, was to discontinue processing employee donations through United Way. Even though employees could donate to any eligible US-based 501(c)(3) nonprofit organization in the late 1990s, the money was still processed by United Way and employees paid a pass-through fee. Employees expected their entire donation to go directly to the nonprofit of their choice and not to have to pay this fee. This decision meant that Microsoft started picking up the processing fees. The company was increasing its financial participation in the giving program and increasing employee trust that their donations were having maximal impact.

The third major decision was to extend the employee match to a year-round match. This meant that employees did not have to wait until October to donate and have their donations matched. Now, employees could plan their donations based on their financial cycles and respond to the needs of the nonprofits they supported. Emergencies do not wait, and employees wanted to respond and have their match sent right away. I remember in 2001, when the Gujarat earthquake struck on January 26, many in the Indian community got mobilized to raise funds to support the victims and recovery effort. My wife, Alka Badshah, was then at Microsoft coordinating the effort there. She had to get special permission from Community Affairs for the donations to be matched immediately and not have to wait till October. This experience was still fresh when Passman joined in 2002, and she got the leadership to agree to extend the employee match to a year-round match.

Bill Gates, in his 1997 memo launching the employee giving campaign for that year, increased the employee match from $10,000 to $12,000. It remained at that level till 2013, when it was increased to $15,000, where it now stands.

A Month of Madness

October is Giving Campaign Month at Microsoft. Employee-driven groups create fundraising campaigns; volunteer at events; hold bake sales; create cat and dog calendars; and create and sell employee cookbooks and photography books. They become involved in a 5K race, a car show, golf tournaments, and an auction. In the past, Bill Gates offered dinner at his house, which he enjoyed hosting. "It was a nice kind of personal thing that you can't buy anywhere else; so, people paid a lot of money and not feel they had overpaid," says Gates. Steve Ballmer hosted a pickup basketball game. Both Gates and Ballmer were the top auction items. The auction alone last year raised more than $2.3 million.

Gates remembers the various events that made the month of October exciting, including the dunking tank where senior executives would sit over a tank of water and employees would throw baseballs to dunk them. "It was all about making events relevant to employees and fun," he says. According to Brad Smith, "It's like the equivalent of . . . the fall football season or the spring parties on university campuses." It brings employees from different parts of the company together and helps develop the culture of the company.

For Gates, the payroll deduction was a big factor in driving increased participation and giving. "It's a heck of a tactic; it didn't feel as large of a gift, you know, a per paycheck kind of a thing." He was wistful that payroll deduction did not catch on in other technology companies as it did at Microsoft.

Kevin Espirito joined Microsoft in his midtwenties in 2000 after being a vendor for the company for a year. At his first one-on-one meeting with his manager, he was excited to share his four written pages of genius—the perfect strategy and plan for his project. His manager cut him off after the first few sentences. His ideas were great, the manager said, but the first one-on-one meeting was about what Microsoft does for the community, about the employee giving program, and identifying what Espirito was passionate about and how the company would support him in that giving. Initially, Espirito was upset that his manager was essentially asking him for money.

The conversation, however, stuck with Espirito. He saw the importance to his manager and the group, so he volunteered for the giving campaign. What Espirito witnessed during that time changed not only his outlook on philanthropy but his idea on what he was personally able to do, considering he had come from a background in which his family had benefited from some of these community services. For the first time in his life, Espirito was in a position not only to make an impact but to double that impact because the company supported his efforts. This eventually led to him becoming the VP appointed lead (VPAL), an employee volunteer for the giving campaign.

As Espirito took on bigger roles in the company, he saw his impact as a VPAL continue to grow. His experience with the giving campaign also mirrored his journey in the company. Microsoft employees have the autonomy to decide how to undertake a project and then bring the approach back to the group for discussion. For Espirito, the giving campaign operated in a similar way: employees invested their time in projects they cared about and were then supported by the company. This decentralized approach, compressed in a one-month campaign period, made it possible for every employee, if they chose, to participate and become engaged in a cause in support of the larger community.

Employees Lead

Microsoft's giving program has become deeply intertwined with the company's culture by being run in large part by employees who serve in key roles. The hundreds of employee volunteers have allowed the program to scale, diversify, and reach across the globe.

There are two programs that help scale the employee giving campaign and keep it running like a well-oiled machine. The VPALs are some 400 employees each year who agree to lead volunteer efforts for their teams around the United States, creating events, selecting causes to support, and surveying their peers to see where their passions and talents lie. They also recruit virtual teams: in 2019, approximately three thousand employees volunteered to scale the October campaign.

"They are the lifeblood," says Karen Bergin, senior director, Microsoft Philanthropies, who now manages the employee giving campaign. "VPALs and other campaign volunteers do this on top of their day jobs for reasons that are as diverse as our employee base. One of our most prolific VPALs is a mother who was a recipient of our giving program; so this is her way to give back to the organization that at one time gave her a helping hand."

Espirito eventually came to work for me and became the manager of the giving campaign. Before joining my team, Espirito was a loaned professional (LP) for the giving campaign. In the loaned professional program, six to eight Microsoft employees take a four-month leave from their regular jobs to help run the giving program during the months leading up to October. These LPs support the VPALs, make connections to nonprofits, and help arrange events from gigantic to modest—all in a whirlwind quarter when they learn how to run key components of the giving campaign while they do it.

Personal stories about why people volunteer or give, stories many employees eventually begin to tell one another, ricochet around the company. In many ways, these stories play a key role in engaging more employees in some aspect of the giving program, said Dave Barnett, a program manager who manages the LPs. "Anyone can buy a cupcake," he said. "But the deeper motivations are what drive people to really make an impact. It becomes contagious."

Espirito made an immediate impact by leading the employee giving team. First, he urged an increase in the match from $12,000 to $15,000 and then made the case to Lisa Brummel, the then chief people officer, to increase the volunteer matching program known as "dollars for doers," from $10 per hour to $17 per hour match for the organization. When employees volunteered a minimum of ten hours for a nonprofit, they would earn a $17 per hour match for the organization. The volunteer time match has now increased to $25 per hour, and they have also got rid of the ten-hour minimum to encourage any level of volunteering. To keep the momentum of this movement going, Microsoft continues to evolve the program and increase its accessibility to even more employees. The program expanded to include interns in 2014 whose donations were matched up to $1,000. In 2019, even interns became eligible to donate up to $15,000 if they choose to, and also started receiving the $50 new hire credit. In 2019, employee participation in the giving program rose to 77 percent, and total dollars to over twenty-three thousand nonprofits increased $14 million from the prior year.

Until recently, Mary Snapp headed Microsoft Philanthropies, an expansion from Community Affairs to lead the company's philanthropic efforts. Mary joined the company in 1988 as Microsoft's first female attorney and has experienced the evolution of the Microsoft employee giving campaign over the past thirty years. For her, the giving campaign was all about team building: "At the time, it was a friendly competition among various teams at Microsoft as a way to build culture in the team, build morale at scale, and raising money was very immature. It was goofy stuff like various tournaments, and teams that lost had to have their executives swim in the lake. I remember Steve Ballmer being in the lake one time."

Snapp goes on to say, "However, for a lot of people like me, the most important thing was that the 'employee benefit' allowed employees to pick the nonprofits of their choice. No way Microsoft otherwise would have supported for example the St. Mary's Catholic School in Newton, Kansas or . . . PETA! And in those days, for many of us still early in our careers, and in my case with law school debt, no way I could have doubled the gift on my own. I maxed out my match every year!"

The giving campaign has grown from an exercise in creating teams and having fun to becoming interwoven with the cultural mission of the company. According to Snapp, "We've become so flexible in the ways that we invite people to give and so nimble responding to causes people care about that we are actually attracting purpose-driven employees to work at this company because of the history, legacy, and the strength of the giving program." Even Pamela Passman expressed the same sentiment that she saw the employee engagement program as a great recruiting tool.

The Great Equalizer

"It is meaningful to be at a mission-driven company where part of that empowerment is through giving—it's through philanthropy. It is this altruistic mission, beyond improving the pocket of our shareholders and ourselves, [that] is really important and really valuable," says Andrea Houchens. After completing her MBA, Houchens wanted to be part of a corporate environment after spending five years as a high school English teacher, so she joined the company in 2017. As she was interviewing, Houchens noticed that many companies mentioned social good as part of their mission. But she found that the Microsoft program was more developed. It was embedded in the company's culture, and there was a lot of enthusiasm around giving at Microsoft. "I feel Microsoft can provide a balance between career trajectory and doing good socially," she says. "I don't have to compromise one or the other, so I can do my job and also focus on philanthropy and still get altruistic satisfaction."

Right after she joined the company, Houchens had an opportunity to work on a giving campaign when she was asked to volunteer during a conference her group was organizing. She coordinated a blood drive, and more than two hundred people donated blood. Houchens is an excellent example of someone who has fully benefited from the employee giving campaign. She now works remotely as a partner development manager covering the mid-Atlantic region from her home in Delaware. As a VPAL, she led her group during the 2018 GIVE campaign, which was about a three month commitment. She has leveraged her experience of working remotely—constantly mobilizing people around her business goals—to mobilize increased participation in the giving campaign.

The giving campaign is about improving social mobility and coming together. "It doesn't matter if you are an engineer, in sales, an executive, or new to the company," she says. "The giving campaign is a great equalizer; it brings humanity back into your job." The giving campaign helps create empathy among employees and connects them with people with whom they would not ordinarily contact. It also helps build employees' networks and provides a different platform to build relationships based not on a bottom line but on service. Collaborating with colleagues in a service activity reveals new dimensions of personalities, thereby building empathy and extending a purpose mindset.

Microsoft continues to grow and evolve the great giving machine. According to Bergin, "We run our giving program like a business. World-class givers deserve a world-class program." Therefore, the team is strategic, analyzing the best time of the best day to email employees about giving opportunities and benefits or conducting surveys about which activities to add. The team remains flexible to highlight the causes that employees rank most important to them (currently education and humanitarian issues).

The giving program has continued to raise more money every year. Snapp was particularly proud that, in 2017, $3.7 million was raised through employee giving and company matching for natural disasters, including Hurricanes Maria, Harvey, and Irma; the California wildfires; and the earthquake in Ecuador. Even during the great recession, when corporate giving overall was down, the giving program continued to grow, and that is because of the continuous improvements, small and major expansions, to ensure employees have the best opportunity to participate. The "dollars for doers" program was added to encourage newer employees who were not as financially well off since the stock at that time was either flat or declining. To keep the momentum and inculcate new employees into the giving DNA of the company, the "dollars for doers" volunteer match program was introduced so employees could contribute with their time and still see Microsoft funds going to their nonprofits. According to Brad Smith, "It's one of the few things that you can measure with statistical accuracy over many years, especially given the degree to which we've measured both the dollars and dollars per employee and the participation rate. And so, it's not generally, from what I can recall, something that has seen speed spikes and valleys but rather a steady progression and support."

I sat down with Brad Smith, to hear his thoughts on the evolution of the employee giving culture at Microsoft. Smith joined Microsoft in 1993 and became the general counsel and chief legal officer in 2002 when Bill Neukom retired. The giving program has expanded exponentially since he's been there. Smith offers two reasons for this growth. First, a new generation of employees (millennials) is enthusiastic about being at a purpose-driven company. Millennials are embracing the giving program and really connecting their own sense of purpose to the company's broader purpose. Second, the giving program has become deeply connected to Microsoft's culture.

Under the leadership of CEO Satya Nadella, the employee giving program has continued to grow and expand. Nadella introduced the one-week hackathon celebration, instead of the traditional company meeting, where employees from all over the company come together to work on creating solutions using technology. "The hackathon is a way to celebrate, break down barriers, increase cross-group collaboration, and of course find inspiration for the other weeks of the year for the work we do here and to exercise the sense of purpose," says Nadella. The hackathon has become a pillar of Microsoft culture, and it is a perfect incubator for both a growth and purpose mindset. It is the largest private hackathon, according to Karen Bergin. The employee engagement team has also extended the hackathon to the nonprofit community by creating a "Hack for Good," where employees create technology solutions for the nonprofit community.

There were a hundred projects in the Hack for Good in July 2019, all of which involve nonprofits. Employees from those nonprofits came to the Microsoft campus to work with employees during the Hack for Good events. Bergin said many Microsoft employees develop deeper relationships with the nonprofits they meet, which becomes another way for employees to connect to the nonprofit community.

Between 2017 and 2019, Bergin introduced several Hack for Good events—one was also held over St. Patrick's Day weekend, and 110 people came for the hack and stayed all night long. Microsoft employees become closer to the nonprofits and help solve some of their problems while also being exposed to the purpose mindset.

Scaling the Impact

Microsoft's giving program continues to increase dollars, participation, and a "doing good" ethos. It is not easy to turn moments into movements. Microsoft's challenge is to keep momentum as the world evolves, new technologies become available, and as social media continues to change how the younger generation of employees wants to engage and create impact.

In our analysis of the employee giving program, we found that it took four years for an employee to be fully vested in it. Many new employees focus first on understanding their work environment and ensuring they make a business impact. Unlike Mary Snapp or Kevin Espirito, who were quickly drawn into the giving culture because of their personal background, not all new employees see the benefits of the program right away.

In 2013, Microsoft introduced a $50 new hire credit for all new employees at their employee orientation, where the employee giving team talks about opportunities for volunteering and giving. This $50 new hire credit starts them on their giving journey by allowing them to give to their nonprofit of choice. In the early days, less than 50 percent of new employees used the new hire credit. This was just leaving money behind.

The lesson was that just because you give money does not mean people will jump in and participate. Folks need other motivations, and to keep the culture of the giving movement thriving, we had to make new efforts to engage employees. In 2019, 76.2 percent of new employees used their $50 new hire credit. By continuing to message effectively, Bergin and her team are keeping employees excited about participating and increasing employee participation. The giving team has also made volunteering easier for employees by increasing options for "microvolunteering."

Bergin and her colleagues knew many employees wanted to volunteer but had trouble finding the time. They solved this problem by introducing microvolunteering, what Bergin describes as "snackable" volunteerism. During a microvolunteering event, a nonprofit comes to campus, and then Microsoft employees have the option of helping with a task for sixty to ninety minutes of their own personal time. For example, in October 2018, the retail store leadership team packed fifteen thousand American Red Cross "comfort kits" during a seventy-five-minute microvolunteering session. While employees packed kits, a Red Cross senior leader talked about how these kits, which included items like soap, razors, and combs, might be used by someone experiencing a disaster like a home fire.

Microsoft is also making it easier for employees to use their professional skills to benefit others, creating a year-round, innovative culture of volunteerism. Bergin intentionally speaks of employee giving as a *program* rather than as a *campaign*. During Microsoft's early years, it matched donations only during October, and the giving program was known as the October Giving Campaign. Microsoft eventually adopted year-round matching, but it still only solicited funds from employees in October. When Bergin took over her current role as director of employee engagement in 2016, there was still a focus on October. She saw this as unsustainable, particularly because of the pressure on her team. Her team transitioned to a year-round cadence. Starting with Martin Luther King Jr. Day in January to the Hack for Good in July, employees apply their skills in ways that add value to nonprofits throughout the year.

One way to engage employees is to offer a focus to work on, which helps them understand where, exactly, their donations are going. Bergin offered the example of Plymouth Housing, an organization working to end homelessness in Seattle. In 2018, Plymouth needed 105 refrigerators for a new housing development. So, Bergin's team posted an opportunity to donate to Plymouth Housing for the new refrigerators. The opportunity filled quickly, and many employees gave donations of the full $550 required to purchase one refrigerator. Bergin noted it was fantastic for employees to know that when they funded one refrigerator, Microsoft would fund a second one.

Jim Urbaitis is one of those employees who is highly engaged and motivated by the employee giving campaign. After he joined the Xbox team at the company in 2013, Nadella's culture shift reignited his altruist spirit—a spirit he had nurtured since being raised by a single mom.

Ready to jump in feetfirst, Urbaitis set his eyes on becoming a VP appointed lead. When the opportunity presented itself, he wanted to create opportunities for his team to be engaged in volunteer opportunities throughout the year and not just during October. He focused on creating a program that would educate, empower, and engage his teammates. The microvolunteer program presented him with an opportunity to start monthly events when his teammates could participate in small volunteering efforts. For example, they would spend two hours on a Friday afternoon at a food pantry, like Food Lifeline, or at an urban farm, like Farmer Frog, where they would help at their greenhouse gardens. In addition, he has also designed small volunteer opportunities at their team off-site meetings to keep the cadence of volunteering going.

Over several years, Urbaitis has grown the employee participation rate for this group from 38 percent to more than 80 percent. Quite an amazing achievement. "It just goes back to my upbringing," he says. "We did not have a lot, but my mom always encouraged us to give back. Now I am in this company that prioritizes giving back and then rewards you with matching your time and money—how cool is that?"

Urbaitis wants to ensure his two daughters have a similar upbringing, one that instills a sense of purpose. Though they are growing up in a wealthy community, they are participating alongside him in his efforts to make a difference. "My daughter just turned six, and she cannot wait to go volunteer with me at Food Lifeline," he says.

As the employee giving program continues to evolve, it's on track to reach $2 billion of total dollars given (including match) in 2020. It reached $1 billion in 2012 and $1.6 billion in 2017. Kate Behncken, the new head of Microsoft Philanthropies, was particularly proud that in the 2019 calendar year 77 percent of Microsoft employees made donations or volunteered. The employee volunteer numbers were also up, with 37 percent of employees contributing 825,000 volunteer hours. And the total raised was another record of $181 million including Microsoft match, supporting over twenty-three thousand nonprofits and schools in the United States and nonprofits serving other countries.

I interviewed Behncken in late March during the COVID-19 lockdown in Seattle, and I wanted to know how the employees were responding. "There is nothing quite as unifying as a global pandemic," she said. "And we have had an incredible response. We have already surpassed the fundraising efforts for Hurricanes Harvey and Maria. I continue to be surprised as people are reaching out to me and other leaders in the company as to what more they can do."

At the core of this program are the thousands of stories of people following their purpose and what impact those acts are having. One employee put it best: "When you're working on something that your heart is fully into, the magic you make, the people you can help, and the things you can get done are incredible. . . . After I volunteer, I have the feeling of wanting to take that back to my day job and mimic that experience, to replicate that energy and excitement at my job. The energy is still inside of you."

Giving History

Microsoft Philanthropies. Re-created by Ada Gupta—RedAlkemi

FIGURE 2

Going Global

Pamela Passman joined Microsoft in 1996 to lead the Asia legal and corporate affairs team, and to be based in Tokyo. As she was aware of the employee matching program, she asked whether an American working overseas would be eligible for this benefit. This benefit, however, could not be extended outside the United States for several reasons. She wondered, "How does this translate into what employees outside of the United States think about their role in philanthropy and the company's role in supporting it?" She quickly learned that philanthropy is very different in different cultures.

When Passman was named the deputy general counsel for corporate and regulatory affairs in 2002 and began to manage the philanthropy team, she would occasionally hear from employees who wanted to extend the employee matching program overseas. In 1999, during the height of the Kosovo crisis, Microsoft employees in Paris discussed the unfolding refugee crisis unfolding in that Serbian province in the Balkan region.

Hundreds of thousands of ethnic Albanians fled violent conflict with Serbian troops. Frank Schott, who worked in the Paris office, recalls his discussion with the UN High Commission for Refugees about how Microsoft employees could help with a new refugee tracking system UNHCR was developing. "With hundreds of thousands of refugees, there was a very real need to get these people into a system, because having eight hundred thousand pieces of paper sitting around wasn't a very efficient way to run the operation," Schott said.

Working with UNHCR, Microsoft employees developed the Refugee Field Kit, which provided displaced people new, official identity cards and an easier method for finding family members. In addition to the almost sixty Microsoft employees who volunteered to work on the project—representing twelve subsidiaries throughout Europe—the group also raised more than $3.5 million in cash and software from Microsoft. They also secured equipment from Microsoft partners, such as Hewlett-Packard and Compaq, among others. Over the years, the Refugee Field Kit has been updated, refined, and used in multiple crises.[5]

The employee volunteering effort during the Kosovo crisis was a major moment for the company and its employees, who saw firsthand how their technology and know-how could help people in crisis. Microsoft employees have continued to step up to provide their talent and solve many challenging situations.

In 2005, Microsoft India launched their employee matching program under the leadership of Ravi Venkatesan, chairman of Microsoft India, and Srini Koppolu, who headed the Microsoft India Development Center (MSIDC). Koppolu had moved from the US to lead the new Hyderabad India Development Center and worked with the leadership to design a local program like the US-based employee benefit. They started with a 250,000-rupee match (a reasonable sum for India) but limited the match to a few organizations, which soon expanded as more employees became familiar with this benefit and continued to utilize it. With the 2016 rule for corporations in India to invest 2 percent of their profits to nonprofits, the scale of the India program is growing. They have also adopted the VPAL model to encourage employees to participate and avail themselves of the match.

Combining Passion with Technology

Anil Bhansali joined MSIDC in 2004, and took over the role of managing director in 2013. The employee giving program grew organically as the India office continued to incorporate best practices from the United States. In 2013, Bhansali, with his corporate social responsibility committee, decided to expand the program and introduced an employee volunteering effort where employees could contribute with their talent and expertise.

Bhansali wanted to go beyond the onetime annual giving program model to create opportunities for employees to be engaged on a sustainable basis. Rather than "Give money, and then I am done," he says, he wanted to "do something where we could put the collective power of Microsoft to create sustained impact." An area of focus for this giving was vision impairment. There are 217 million people who have moderate or severe distance vision impairment, and many could avoid impairment if they have access to early diagnosis and treatment.[6] Bhansali and team decided they would take on certain projects where they could make a significant impact. The MSIDC office in Hyderabad partnered with the local L. V. Prasad Eye Institute to launch a mobility and sensory stimulation park and a helpline for the visually impaired. Both projects were funded by contributions from the employee giving campaign at MSIDC. The park is one of the rarest in the world and provides a unique opportunity by exposing the visually challenged to nonvisual sensory experiences such as touch, hearing, smell, taste, and residual vision. The park is also expected to improve body posture, manual dexterity, mental abilities, and communication and socialization skills.[7]

In 2016, the partnership with L.V. Prasad Eye Institute deepened with the launch of Microsoft Intelligent Network for Eyecare (MINE). "By using the power of cloud and pioneering work in the field of AI and ML, along with the knowledge of global experts in ophthalmology, we aimed at bringing preventive and more accessible eyecare to the community," says Bhansali.[8]

As mentioned above, with the 2 percent corporate social responsibility law, which mandates large companies to spend at least 2 percent of their profits every year on CSR projects,[9] the amount Microsoft must spend in

India on CSR projects also increased substantially, and the contributions raised from the employee giving campaign were not enough. The expansion of the vision impairment project was an interesting way to marry the power of technology to purpose. Employees are motivated to apply the technology they are developing for business purposes and extend that to a deeper and sustained societal impact.

MSIDC has continued to explore other opportunities to apply the power of technology to education, agriculture, and health. The art of traditional weaving and handloom textiles is under threat all over the world. In India itself, there are more than 470 traditional handloom clusters that are unable to sustain livelihoods due to their unorganized nature, dispersed structure, inadequate working capital, dilapidated infrastructure, poor institutional framework, lack of education among workers, and dissociation from modern technologies. Bhansali and his team saw an opportunity to combine the training programs that Microsoft had launched globally, and he revived some of these forgotten indigenous handloom forms through the application of technology.

Bhansali believes that by partnering with other organizations, companies, governments, and nonprofits one can start chipping away at major societal problems that face India and other parts of the world. "By continually looking at opportunities where we can have a deep impact through our technology and combine it with our employee's passion and purpose, we can have a lasting impact," he says.

The Microsoft Giving benefit differs from market to market, based on local leadership decisions. Many subsidiaries fund their own programs, and others, such as Canada, India, and the UK, offer a matching benefit. Karen Bergin has been working to create increased uniformity around the world, such as the recent 'Give Together' campaign which proved to be very successful, resulting in millions of dollars going to nonprofits responding to COVID-19. She works with international colleagues to help them increase volunteerism in their markets through approaches such as mentoring, microvolunteering, and participation in Hack for Good. Other changes she implemented include the rollout of a giving-tool platform in 2018 alongside a global 'Give' brand with comprehensive Marcom support and collateral. The area she focuses on is fast sharing of best practices so that subsidiaries can quickly learn from each other and replicate what works for their local markets.

Small Teams Make a Big Impact

The loaned professional program is the secret sauce for the growing success of the employee giving campaign. Six to eight employees are loaned to the philanthropy team to help run the employee giving campaign over four months. "The giving season starts in September as part of the United Way Day of Caring (where employees from companies around Seattle take the day off to volunteer on specific projects). [Then it] goes through the giving campaign and then ends with the giving trees," says Jaime Weber, who served as a loaned professional in the 2017 campaign. Weber has served in multiple roles over her seven years at Microsoft, from helping organize the Day of Caring activity for her team, serving as a VPAL, and finally serving as a loaned professional.

This small team is responsible for all aspects of the giving campaign: creating marketing materials, supporting the VPALs in creating specific events, creating guidelines and policies (the dos and don'ts of a giving campaign), and executing some of the more prominent companywide activities, such as the auction. "This is all about educating and motivating employees about celebrating the culture of giving at Microsoft," she says. Webber works in commercial business, helping large enterprises to empower their people to effectively use Microsoft's technology. She loves her work and helping companies and the business, but she also loves the fact that she can work with nonprofits and the community to fulfill her personal purpose. "Working as a loaned professional was a highlight of my career, for sure," she says, "because it is a small group of people supporting employees' passions and empowering them to do good."

Weber worked on creating communication and marketing materials to support some of the events planned for October during the giving campaign. The VPAL celebration at the end of the campaign was one of the highlights because they had the opportunity to give gratitude for all the hard work the VPALs put in to make the campaign successful. It really is just a small group of people who are working across the company to make a huge difference collectively.

I asked Weber what would happen if the giving campaign came to an end. It was hard for her to imagine that, as the campaign has become so ingrained in the DNA of the company. The employee giving program extends the mission of the company to the community at large and allows for employees to discover and apply their purpose, which goes beyond work. That is its greatest achievement.

Lessons for Igniting a Movement

The employee giving program exists within a much larger and broader effort on the part of the company to create societal value. This is not unique to Microsoft, but the three CEOs—Bill Gates, Steve Ballmer, and Satya Nadella—have each supported and driven this sense of mission in different ways.

The employee giving campaign fits Microsoft's broader corporate responsibility approach to society and the community in which it operates. In its 2018 corporate social responsibility report, Microsoft stated: "We work to apply the power of technology to empower people, strengthen communities, and protect our planet. Our business practices and policies reflect our commitment to making a positive impact around the globe. This commitment impacts the products and services we develop and is central to why many of our employees come to work every day."[10] The three areas in which they report are: empowering people, strengthening communities, and protecting our planet.

Microsoft employees find purpose in multiple aspects of their connections to the company. According to Brad Smith, there are three main "pillars of purpose" at Microsoft. The first and most important pillar is the sense of purpose that employees get from their day jobs, the products they work on, and the customers they serve. This is why people come to work and where they spend most of their time. Second, many employees find meaning and purpose in their connections with other employees. Special events like hackathons break down barriers between teams and give employees opportunities to connect on projects that go beyond their daily work. The employee giving program is the third pillar of purpose that connects the company with all its US employees, and it also drives the company's culture.

Since 1983, when the initial payroll deduction program began, the great giving machine continues to grow. This is because employee engagement and employee giving are treated as a campaign with a sustained effort, supported not only at the highest level but at all levels. It is now part of the company's DNA. When I spoke to Bill Hilf, CEO of Vulcan (Paul Allen's companies and enterprises, profiled in chapter 5), he shared that it had been an honor to lead the giving campaign for the Windows server business he was responsible for. "I had to get a giant division to catalyze the teams and do all of the reporting, etc.," he said. "It was one of the most enjoyable parts of my Microsoft journey, and I had a full-time job on top of that."

Arpita Agarwal—the cofounder of MAQ software (profiled in chapter 3)—has a similar recollection of the giving campaign. According to Arpita, the giving campaign allowed her to get involved, without being forced, as there were multiple avenues to participate in. She, too, remembers the feeling of honor and privilege to participate in the giving campaign and give back to the community. She recalled her vice president telling their whole group why participating in the giving campaign and getting involved was a privilege.

The employee giving program is also successful because:

1. The program continuously evolves to meet where employees want to go and creates opportunities that allow them to thrive. Providing employees with an opportunity to use their time, talent, and treasure is critical. Several elements were introduced: opportunities for employees to serve on nonprofit boards and to train them how to serve effectively; an online tool to help employees discover volunteer opportunities easily; and the microvolunteering program. All of these have gone a long way to build that culture of purpose.

2. A strong operational system has been created that ensures employee money flows and is distributed in small amounts to

thousands of nonprofits around the world. It is not easy moving money in this way, given numerous national and local government regulations and laws. These laws also change, and one must ensure a strict compliance policy. Further, the operational program also evolved to serve the employees in the most effective way, switching from United Way processing the match and charging a fee to employees to Microsoft picking up the costs of processing the fees and moving to an outside vendor as the program grew; and finally moving to another vendor that could offer the best technology to meet the current needs. These moves are very challenging as they have to be done without any hiccups in the employees' contributions and their match.

3. The messaging of the program has also evolved over the years. What started off as fun competition between various groups and divisions developed into a very competitive effort. Employees felt they were encouraged to participate, as groups wanted to have the highest participation rate or most money raised. Eventually, the competition aspect of the program was dialed back as it was getting some negative feedback, and new incentives were added to keep the program growing, such as the dollars-for-doers program.

4. The program offerings have continuously evolved to match changing employee needs. Rather than focus on just one month of giving, more microvolunteering opportunities and the Hack for Good were added over the course of the year. For the continued success of any such effort, it is critical the program continues to evolve.

A moment inspired by Mary Gates and launched formally by Bill Neukom has turned into a movement that continues to grow, inspiring employees, providing them with unique opportunities both inside and outside of their jobs to find purpose. In doing so, the movement has impacted the well-being of thousands of nonprofit organizations and transformed the lives of millions of individuals around the world. "Giving at

Microsoft is like getting up in the morning and having coffee. It's habit forming, and I have never seen anything like this. I can mark my years at Microsoft by the giving campaign," says Nadella.

This is an untold story of the impact of Microsoft, its employees, and its alumni. They have effectively combined a growth mindset, which brings value in their work and to their customers, with a purpose mindset and extended the impact and benefits to people all over the world.

Richard Kaplan is the general manager of employee experience at Microsoft, and his group is responsible for the end-to-end journey of an employee. In his role, he meets with new employees regularly and he reminds them of Microsoft's mission, which is to "empower every person and every organization on the planet to do more." And he reminds them how the company provides a platform through its matching gifts platform to enable every employee to do just that. "Those who are joining Microsoft more than anything want to make a difference in the world. Microsoft's mission gives them that purpose at work, and the employee giving campaign extends that purpose outside of work," says Kaplan. He also chats with alumni, and one aspect of the company they miss most is the matching gifts program, because of the enormous impact it has in the community.

Microsoft is continuing to evolve and grow its programs and launching new opportunities to have even greater impact. "I think we have an incredible opportunity to extend the global impact of the giving program with our employees around the world," says Kate Behncken. Her team is focused on issues surrounding equity, critical humanitarian needs, doing more to help people develop skills for employability, local social and economic impact initiatives in strategic communities, and empowering nonprofits and humanitarian organizations with technology to accelerate social impact. Locally, in the Puget Sound region, Microsoft is focused on addressing homelessness and affordable housing issues. "This creates opportunities to think about creative ways that we can engage our employees in the giving campaign, to volunteer for the different initiatives that the company is focused on," says Behncken.

According to Gates, "I am very proud of the fact that people have taken their analytical capabilities and the wealth they have gotten from Microsoft, and the understanding, and applied it in such a creative way to philanthropy. Philanthropy is very fulfilling, and I do think the giving campaign played a role in that; and I think the founders being generous helps out with that." He wants more companies to find creative ways to get employees involved in their community: "You get exposure and realize there are some really amazing causes out there; you see other people doing it; and you thank God, you know, that there's a moral purpose more than just my normal job."

In the following chapters, you will be introduced to several changemakers starting with Jeff and Tricia Raikes, Paul and Yaffa Maritz, Nathan Myhrvold, and Jean-Phillipe Courtois who have taken their wealth and combined their growth and purpose mindsets to drive societal change and invest in the common good. You will also hear from early Microsoft alumni who left the company to pursue their purpose and increase the well-being of their communities, as well as from more recent alumni and current employees who continue to build on this culture of giving and investing their time, talent, and treasure for the common good.

CHAPTER TWO

The Origin Story

n the late nineteenth century, the use of corporate funds for philanthropy was illegal, an almost unimaginable idea in today's world. Business professor Mark Sharfman has traced the evolution of corporate
philanthropy, describing how society's views on business and its role in
society have evolved to our contemporary moment, where corporate
philanthropy is an expected contribution from businesses.[1]

Even though judicial precedent limited the charitable activities of corporations during the last quarter of the nineteenth century, companies
still found ways to make contributions to social causes through funding
local schools, libraries, and even the YMCA. Though these contributions
often had mixed benefits for communities, we can see the earliest glimpse
of corporate philanthropy philosophies in these projects.[2]

Company towns were examples where corporations helped fund local
schools, libraries, and so on that were located on their premises; the Pull-
man Company is an illustration of that. The railways supported the Young
Men's Christian Association (YMCA) to establish facilities at railroad

terminals with the railroads paying for 60 percent of the operating costs and the railroads' employees making up the remainder.[3] The argument was that the investment was business related because railroad employees needed a place to stay. Not all examples of corporate philanthropy led to an unqualified pubic good; some of these efforts were seen as an extension of slavery.[4] But what I am describing is how companies can move away from a paternalistic attitude and cultivate the individual, collective interaction of employees that leads to genuine altruism.

Today, employee giving and volunteering is almost a public expectation for major companies, though some companies like Amazon are outliers. (Even Amazon, though, is developing other programs to support the community in which they have their footprint.) As a young technology company in the 1980s, Microsoft became a leader in how it established its employee giving and philanthropy program, as I discussed in the previous chapter. In this chapter, I retell the stories of early Microsoft employees and the impact the employee giving campaign had on their own personal development and growth and how that led to them creating a culture of service and giving and developing a purpose mindset. The United Way of King County has played a very important role in providing the training for so many of the early employees to learn and get engaged in the community, which allowed those employees to extend their growth mindset into a purpose mindset.

The First Couple

Tricia and Jeff Raikes became the first Microsoft couple to get married. Tricia's mother instilled the value of showing up in their Seattle community. "My mother was an incessant volunteer," she says. Though they had a modest income, her family was always volunteering and raising funds for community nonprofit organizations, including the United Way, the Heart Association, or the March of Dimes. "Back in those days, you raised funds going door to door; as a little girl, I walked alongside her, and my job was to carry the white envelopes," says Tricia. Giving back was just expected— an expectation Tricia (née McGinnis) has carried with her throughout her life.

Jeff Raikes grew up on a Nebraska farm between Lincoln and Omaha, and went to school in a small farming community of two thousand that helped him develop a deep sense of community. His parents also instilled the importance of community involvement; his mother was always running a Red Cross event, and his father worked on agricultural issues important to all farmers. Jeff recounts a story that has stayed with him since that time: "I was probably twelve or thirteen years old. There was a blizzard in Nebraska, and we heard a knock on the door. A couple whose car had gotten stuck in the snowdrift was asking for help. It was about twelve below zero, and my father was quick to volunteer me. He asked me to get the tractor and chain. Together, my dad and I pulled the couple out of the snowdrift. They were eager to give my dad some money in appreciation, and my dad politely declined. He expressed his hope that if one of his children was in need at some point in the future, he hoped somebody would step up to help them. That was my first lesson about paying it forward."

Jeff jokes about moving from the farm in Nebraska to the farm at Stanford University, where he was introduced to and then became involved in the African American community there. "It was strange that a white farm boy from Nebraska would get immersed in black culture and live at an African American–themed dorm." His roommate also grew up not too far from Jeff in North Omaha, just thirty-five minutes away. His urban neighborhood was the cultural inverse of Jeff's all-white farming community. This experience opened Jeff's eyes to the issues of social injustice in the United States. "My experiences at Stanford stuck with me throughout my life and influenced our philanthropic and impact pursuits, including a focus on equity and racial justice," he says.

Early Giving

Tricia Raikes was employee number seventy-five when she joined Microsoft in July 1981 to build the marketing and communication function for the company. Jeff joined a few months later in November. Tricia was excited to work with passionate, smart people, all oriented towards the aspiration of Microsoft's vision of "a computer on every desk and in every home." Many of her friends thought she was crazy since most did not know what "software" meant. Despite enjoying her work, she says, "there was a piece of me that needed to be fulfilled, and that was about giving back to the community and being active in the community."

She was blessed to be at a company whose cofounder also had incredible community-engaged parents. Mary Gates (Bill's mother) took a few of the women managers under her wing. She inspired and ignited Tricia Raikes's interests and connected her with her first board opportunity at the Kirkland and Redmond Boys and Girls Club. This was even before the employee giving campaign began. Tricia had been launched on a trajectory of deep engagement in the community and the eventual establishment of the Raikes Foundation.

Bill Gates has said in many forums that his job was to concentrate on Microsoft and build great software. His parents, Bill Sr. and Mary Gates, were the role models who planted the early seeds of philanthropy and built the culture of giving back at Microsoft. Both Bill Sr. and Mary Gates were deeply engaged in the United Way, which was well established in the broader Seattle business community. Mary Gates was also on the board of the national United Way and was instrumental in eventually launching the United Way payroll deduction program in 1983 (see chapter 1).

Jeff and Tricia Raikes were also instrumental in motivating and inspiring early Microsoft employees to be involved in the community and to learn how to get started with philanthropy. They recounted a time when they were invited by Mary and Bill Sr. for a weekend brunch with Warren and Susie Buffett, as well as with Bill Gates and Ann Winblad (the founder of Hummer Winblad Venture Partners). Tricia recalls Mary Gates asking her to speak about how it was to step out of the workplace as an up-and-coming manager and to deploy her skills in the philanthropic space. For Tricia, this meeting highlighted the various ways individuals can actively engage in community, through the company, or directly with community partners. This also validated the work she was embarking on.

The Role Models

When Microsoft went public in 1986, the Raikes' financial status shifted markedly. Jeff recalled Warren Buffett telling them a few years later, "You want your kids to have enough money so they can do anything but not so much that they choose to do nothing." Inspired in part by Buffett's comment, there was never any question in their mind that the lion's share of their wealth would be returned to society. Their responsibility now was to learn, as first-generation philanthropists, and decide how to do that in a way that would have the greatest impact.

Tricia and Jeff were indebted in this respect to their great role models, Mary Gates, Bill Gates Sr., Warren Buffett, and Susie Buffett, for giving them insights and guidance as they embarked on their philanthropy. Mary Gates was particularly instrumental in reaching out and helping Tricia pursue her interest in connecting to early leadership roles in the community.

The Microsoft giving campaign was also instrumental in shaping their philanthropy. The campaign expanded their understanding of giving and how to utilize their time, talent, and capital effectively. Moreover, it gave them practice in being curious about community challenges by being near these challenges as volunteers. "We were committed to learning about and supporting work in our community and felt a deep responsibility to do it well," says Tricia.

When Tricia left Microsoft in 1988 to raise her family, she became deeply involved in the community, eventually becoming the chair of the board of the Redmond and Kirkland Boys and Girls Club. Jeff says with a sense of pride that, during her tenure, the Redmond and Kirkland Boys and Girls Club became one of the largest chapters in the country.

As Raikes continued his rise at Microsoft in his capacity as the executive leading Microsoft North America, he recalls a 1994 visit to the Boston sales office, where he learned about an organization called NFTE (National Foundation for Training Entrepreneurship). Raikes was fascinated by how the Boston team had bonded and was committed to this organization, which trained youth from disadvantaged circumstances to become entrepreneurs. Raikes took this approach and shared it as a model for the rest of the sales offices across the United States; ultimately, most of the sales offices began working with NFTE. Raikes also helped develop an online NFTE curriculum and helped them evolve their business model so they could scale and reach more youth. I remember Jeff asking me to get engaged when I joined Microsoft, and my team eventually offered support to NFTE through a national grant. "In this particular case, I got that visceral feeling, that deep sense, of how powerful it was to create an opportunity for employees to engage in the community across the country, to engage in their community," says Jeff. Community engagement became a powerful element in building a culture at Microsoft, and Jeff Raikes was at the forefront of that effort.

Evolution of the Giving Campaign

Tricia and Jeff were active participants and eventual leaders of the Microsoft employee giving campaign. Their recollections of the early days provide insight into how Microsoft so fully embraced this culture of giving as a young technology company. United Way King County was an established community organization with a workplace giving campaign in many of the prominent companies in the area. Jeff and Tricia recalled that workplace campaigns at Boeing and Weyerhaeuser were much more traditional, with an automatic monthly payroll deduction—there was an expectation to participate. But this contribution at Microsoft was both fun and voluntary.

In the early days, campaigns were set up to be a competition between divisions. "Microsoft was bringing more of its retail mentality and its campaign orientation to bear," says Tricia. "The company's intent was to introduce a young employee population to the importance of giving back – and to do it by having fun and tapping their competitive spirit." Also, Microsoft's early message was to encourage not only financial contributions but also volunteerism. It was this combination that motivated teams to go out into the community at the United Way Day of Caring. But it was also a valuable learning opportunity.

Microsoft's message of engaging with the community and giving back was a high priority. "For a young tech company so early in its growth, this was extraordinary as well," says Tricia. Microsoft also influenced United Way in return: they shifted their approach to place the intent of the donor squarely at the center of employee giving. In the past, United Way had acted as a conduit that would decide what community efforts and organizations would be supported. Microsoft employees' desire to be involved in directing their philanthropy created some real challenges for United Way. Over time, Microsoft ultimately moved to a more open campaign, where employees could direct their funds to organizations of their choice.

The movement toward an open campaign was certainly positive, as employees had a more active role in deciding where their dollars would go. Jeff, however, felt the pendulum had swung too far and believed that employees should allocate at least a portion of their donation to United Way's "Safety Net," because employees on their own didn't have the time or, likely, the expertise to fully understand the needs of the community.

What remained constant throughout this process was Microsoft leadership's commitment to the employee giving campaign. Jeff recounts a story, now company lore, when Steve Ballmer and Mike Maples (both part of the Office of the President) swam across a small pond on campus affectionately called Lake Bill. The original competition stated that whoever's division lost had to swim across the lake. Both Ballmer and Maples agreed that one division had the highest percentage of participation and the other had the most per capita giving, so they both agreed to swim. "In anticipation of this, the employees had gone and filled up the lake with blocks of ice, so the water was nice and cold," recalls Jeff. Tricia chimes in, "Maples had a wetsuit under his suit and tie, and they both jumped in in their office attire."

Microsoft executives have consistently served on the board of United Way and led the annual United Way fundraising campaign. Jeff and Tricia Raikes led the 2006–7 campaign, raising over $124 million. They have both been actively involved with the United Way, with Tricia having served on the board and both having participated in the "point-in-time count," United Way's annual effort to determine the homeless population in Seattle. They, with hundreds of others, would go out in the middle of the night to count the number of number of people experiencing homeless-ness in Seattle and, in the process, were able to learn more about home-lessness and the myriad systemic failures contributing to the challenge.

Brad Smith, now the president of Microsoft, and his wife, attorney Kathy Surace-Smith, led the 2010–11 campaign, and Chris Capossela, the chief marketing officer and executive vice president, and his wife, Leigh Toner, are leading the 2019–20 campaign. "I can't imagine that there is another company that has this number of their leaders over the years stepping into the broad community leadership," Jeff says. "This really just reinforces the importance of being engaged in the community." Bill and Melinda Gates have also continued to host the annual Tocqueville Society donors, those who consistently contribute $25,000 or more each year.

The Next Phase

The Raikes Foundation, spearheaded by Tricia, was launched in 2002. At the end of 2007, Jeff decided it was time for his life's next chapter. "There was a deep bench already at Microsoft, and they were ready to take on the next level of leadership," says Jeff. "I had three things on my mind. One was working with my brother on international agricultural development, given my farming background; the second was teaching at a business school; and third, which I suggested to Bill Gates, was to support the agri-cultural development program at the Gates Foundation. But in 2008, Bill and Melinda Gates asked me to take over as the chief executive of the Gates Foundation. This was a serendipitous leadership opportunity that I never anticipated, and it gave me an incredible opportunity to learn from a partner with three of the world's greatest philanthropists in Bill and Melinda Gates and Warren Buffett."

Tricia and Jeff's guiding vision is to create a just and equitable future for all young people. "For Jeff and me, the big aspiration is the future state of the world where race, gender, identity, sexual orientation, and socio-economic status, and other markers of social identity do not determine an individual's life outcomes or sense of belonging," Tricia says. "It is a lofty aspiration, but this ethos animates the work we do at our foundation."

Setting a bold vision is not new for Jeff and Tricia, as Microsoft employees are instilled with the idea that they are part of changing the world. "For outsiders, it may come off as arrogant, but with all appropriate humility, we did feel we were part of changing the world," says Jeff. Jeff brought that same spirit when he led the Microsoft Alumni Network to connect alumni around the world. Together, the alumni would help amplify the potential impact of their philanthropy by leveraging each other's experience.

Tricia and Jeff bring these lessons and experiences from Microsoft to their foundation and to all their social impact pursuits more broadly. They apply their growth and purpose mindset to their work: they are big believers in the philanthropy sector, in how they can use their voice for advocacy, and how they can be continuous learners. As we closed our conversation, Tricia spoke about the four principles of their foundation's Impact-Driven Philanthropy initiative: (1) do your homework, (2) it is never too early or too late to start giving back, (3) practice humility, and (4) collaborate and partner with others. "Effective philanthropy takes practice, so engage now and stretch your muscles because you will learn, and you will evolve along the way."

Tricia encourages everyone to start with a beginner, learning mindset and to be a good listener. She also encourages everyone to work with others, as these are significant and complex problems that cannot be addressed adequately by just one organization. "Seek out the voices of those who bring lived experience as they are the experts, join with other like-minded partners, and be mindful when you can bridge to others who may not yet be allies in your work," she says. And finally, she says it is about continuous learning: "You know there is a famous quote that says, 'No battle plan survives first contact with the enemy.'"[5] Develop a strategic plan, but be ready to pivot and be nimble once you're on the field.

The Renaissance Man

At age nine, Nathan Myhrvold cooked a Thanksgiving dinner for his family, but not with family recipes or parental guidance. He found cookbooks at the local library. "When I was a kid, I discovered cookbooks—it was the coolest thing that you could learn how to cook," he says. An incessant reader fascinated by science and math, he began college at UCLA at age fourteen and graduated with a bachelor's degree in mathematics and a master's degree in geophysics and space physics. At Princeton, Myhrvold earned a master's degree in mathematical economics and completed his PhD in theoretical and mathematical physics.

Myhrvold was working under Stephen Hawking as a postdoctoral fellow in physics at Cambridge when he learned about personal computers. Some friends from Princeton had started developing a multitasking software for DOS, so he took a leave of absence to join his friends and became the CEO of Dynamical Systems Research based in Oakland, California. In 1986, Microsoft acquired DSR and Myhrvold because of a director of special projects there. He worked in a variety of executive positions and founded Microsoft Research in 1991. In 1996, Myhrvold became the first chief technology officer.

Myhrvold is a renaissance man with a wide range of interests. He is an amateur paleontologist and has participated on an expedition to hunt for a dinosaur skeleton in eastern Montana. He has funded a dinosaur bone-digging foundation that has recovered more *Tyrannosaurus rex* skeletons than the total previously found by everyone else. He donated most of them to museums, including the Smithsonian. Inside the tall, curved windows of his living room on the shores of Lake Washington, he has a skeleton of a *Tyrannosaurus rex* he helped uncover. He is also a cosmologist, a zoologist, an environmentalist, a photographer, a fossil- and book-collector, and an accomplished cook.[6]

Peering around the Corner

At Microsoft, Myhrvold served as an adviser to Gates and played an important role in many projects, including Microsoft Windows, Windows NT, and Windows CE operating systems. "As any software company," he says, "we were working on things that you're behind on and could not include in the last release. Then you've got things which are coming up in the short term, and they're what everybody in the industry is talking about. And then there are things a little bit further out, and it is very hard to have enough intellectual bandwidth to set aside some time and other needed resources to work on. And then there are things that are a little further out, and it is important be focused on it, and that is what I did."

Microsoft Research is the powerhouse it is today due to this ability to devote the time and intellectual resources required to peer around the corner and glimpse the big picture. It also allowed Myhrvold to work closely with Gates in designing the company's technology strategy.

This same attitude of risk-taking and pushing boundaries also drove Myhrvold as he participated in the employee giving campaign. He offered skydiving, bungee jumping, and parasailing experiences with him to raise money. Myhrvold knew employees were doing well financially and could afford to give some money to charity that would be matched by the company. He offered a startling insight about the brilliance of this workplace campaign: "You have a health plan, you go work out, and you give something to charity," he says.

Myhrvold took time off from Microsoft to get an advanced culinary degree from the esteemed La Varenne in Burgundy. "When I worked at Microsoft, I realized one day that I had lots of formal training on things I did not use all the time, like theoretical physics," he says. "I loved cooking, but I had no formal training, so I went to Bill [Gates] and got him to give me leave of absence to go to cooking school in France, which was a fantastic experience."

Shifting the Trajectory of Innovation

When Myhrvold retired from Microsoft in 1999, he turned his attention to other pursuits, including the creation of Intellectual Ventures and IV Lab—a global business that creates, incubates, and commercializes impactful inventions.[7] At a 2005 reception, I saw Myhrvold and Gates discussing using depleted uranium as fuel to develop smaller nuclear power plants for green energy. Together, as part of IV Lab, they founded Terra-Power to develop a class of nuclear fast reactors called "traveling wave reactors." Global Good, a unit of IV Labs, was created with support from Bill Gates to explore how technology can positively impact the lives of people living on under two dollars a day. Global Good's genesis was the idea that they should tackle thorny problems no one else wanted to address. With this support from Bill Gates, Myhrvold spends his time on these challenging problems that others avoid.

The Institute for Disease Modeling (IDM) is one of the efforts of which he is most proud. I interviewed Myhrvold as COVID-19 had started in China and moved to Seattle. He said, "What we're seeing with this coronavirus is a disease that started with very low-tech roots and jumped to people, and without a vaccine or an effective therapy, it's not that different than combating a virus in the Middle Ages." IDM models infectious diseases around the world, a vital task because diseases have complicated and highly nonlinear means of spreading. It is impossible to effectively control them without a quantitative understanding of what happens as these diseases spread. "It's like running a modern business without any spreadsheets," he says. IDM has already made significant contributions to the polio and malaria campaigns, also a focus of the Bill and Melinda Gates Foundation. IDM has also played an important role in disseminating information for the COVID-19 pandemic.[8]

Another effort is the development of a cervical cancer diagnostic that promises to revolutionize the identification and treatment of cervical cancer around the world. As this technology is being designed keeping in mind countries with few resources, it could save the lives of a billion women. In the United States and other countries with many resources, periodic cervical cancer screenings are routine. But that is not so in many parts of the world. Screenings for cervical cancer are imperative to catch the cancer before it spreads. Not only is the test prototype inexpensive, but the treatment course itself is relatively inexpensive compared to other cancers. "Our test is interesting because I think it will be the first widely deployed use of machine learning for doing a cancer diagnostic, so we're super proud of it," Myhrvold says.

Myhrvold is also very proud of the fact that at Global Good they work in incredibly challenging areas of solving what seems to be intractable problems in places with no resources. He counts his blessings when they have been able to make some contributions. One area that Myhrvold has focused on is the importance of food and cooking as it relates to health.

The Largest Cookbook

Since early childhood, Myhrvold has been fascinated by cooking as a science. "Cooking is very complicated," he explains. "There's a tremendous amount of physics involved. For example, there is the physics of heat transfer. There's also a tremendous amount of chemistry involved. Now, the miracle is our ancestors learned to cook without knowing anything about physics or chemistry; it was a purely empirical approach that worked."

Upon leaving Microsoft, Myhrvold refocused his attention on cooking and published what is probably the world's largest cookbook, *Modernist Cuisine: The Art and Science of Cooking*. The cookbook emerged from a cooking lab he built to experiment with the science of cooking and a whole range of recipes, including traditional favorites. "There were lots of principles of cooking and many were false because no one had tested them," he says. "What this allowed us to do was test lots of these principles and develop recipes to put these ideas into practice."

Myhrvold brings the science lessons of cooking to global challenges. On one side, you have too much food and the problem of overeating and obesity. On the other side, massive numbers of people go hungry. One of the most crucial questions he seeks to answer through his experiments with cooking is how to bridge the divide between the people who are eating too much unhealthy food and the people who are eating too little. Developing nutritious meals for people in rich and poor countries is what he is working on.

These science lessons extend to the effects of malnutrition, which are devastating. A child can recover from starvation with a phenomenon called "catch-up growth"—they might never be tall, but they do catch up. But the long-term cognitive damage is irreversible. This is why the core of Myhrvold's work is to use science to grow more nutritious and delicious food, which consumes fewer natural resources. "Technology cannot solve all of the problems," he says, "and understanding of food can't solve all of these problems. Many of them are a mixture of cultural issues and politics, but we are trying."

Myhrvold reflects on how Microsoft was ridiculed for the aspiration to put a computer on every desk and in every home. "We did it; we did not listen to the naysayers," he says. Myhrvold takes the discipline of confronting seemingly insurmountable challenges he learned at Microsoft and applies it to seemingly intractable global problems. He is working with talented biologists, medical doctors, and other professionals and applying technologies to tackle problems no one else has on their priority list.

The Quiet Philanthropists

Living on a thirty-thousand-acre cattle ranch in Rhodesia (now Zimbabwe) gives you a different sense of the environment and a love of nature. Paul Maritz grew up on such a cattle ranch. After finishing school in South Africa, he traveled to England and then to the United States. He was one of the lucky ones: his parents invested in his education, and through hard work, he secured a job at Intel in 1981. "Intel was a microprocessor semiconductor company, and I was a software guy, so I wanted to work in a software-focused company," says Maritz. After flirting with a start-up, Maritz joined Microsoft in 1986. Microsoft was the first commercial licensee of Unix, which was developed by Bell Labs. But by 1986, Linux was not part of Microsoft's focus. Maritz was hired to lead a team of ten people to decide what to do with Linux.

Fast-forward fourteen years: Maritz had ten thousand people working on his team, and he oversaw all desktop and server software, including such major initiatives as the development of Windows 95, Windows NT, and Internet Explorer. By the time he left the company in 2000, he was the third-ranking executive behind Bill Gates and Steve Ballmer. Maritz recounts that Bill's mother, Mary, served on the national board of the United Way with John Roberts Opel, who was the CEO of IBM at that time. This relationship could be seen as the real beginning of Microsoft, as IBM selected this relatively unknown company to provide an operating system for its computers in 1981.

In hindsight, it is evident that the United Way and its philosophy of giving back to the community was woven into the fabric of Microsoft, which was unique for a small technology company at the time. "It was sort of a friendly rivalry between groups in the company to see who would make greater contributions; senior executives would volunteer to be hu-miliated to motivate the employees to participate," recalls Maritz. As with several other early Microsoft employees, Maritz's stock options continued to increase in value, and he and his wife, Yaffa Maritz, continued to make larger commitments to United Way "because at that time I was working full-time and did not have the time to think about setting up our own philanthropy—United Way provided that vehicle."

Yaffa Maritz, on the other hand, grew more interested in working on issues related to child and family welfare, so she actively participated in United Way and discovered organizations they would support in the fu-ture. Not being from the United States, they felt incredibly lucky to be in the right place at the right time. "Very few people get the opportunity to be part of the birth of a major new industry and see the rewards of that," says Maritz. "We were living the American dream, there was a sense of responsibility to give back, and United Way was our first foray to do so."

Giving versus Leveraged Giving

In 2000, Maritz attended the "Creating Digital Dividends Conference." I attended, too, and remember well the debate emerging between Bill Gates and Mohammed Yunus, founder of Grameen Bank, father of the microlending movement and eventual winner of the Nobel Peace Prize in 2006. Gates argued that if you were living on less than a dollar a day, tech-nology wouldn't be that relevant to your life, while Yunus offered the opposite view. He challenged the tech industry to do something about this apparent lack of relevance. Craig McCaw, the founder of McCaw Cellular, got introduced to Yunus and at the same time offered an initial invest-ment to launch the Grameen Technology Center. Maritz became involved in the Grameen Technology Center and my own nonprofit, Digital Part-ners Foundation.

As someone who worked in the tech industry, Maritz sought ways to ap-ply his money that would have high leverage and a multiplier effect. So Grameen Technology Center and Digital Partners Foundation efforts to apply technology to help the poor made sense to him. But he had also learned over the years that there is value in giving money where there is an immediate need. Maritz's solution was to split his philanthropy by supporting leveraged efforts and giving to people whose lives he could affect directly. "It is one thing to give through organizations and endeavors that give high leverage and it is important," he says. "But it's another thing to give where you can interact directly with people and understand the particulars of people's struggles and their lives." The satisfaction one derives from each approach is different, and it expands different muscles of your system.

Finding Your Sweet Spot

Maritz's effort is focused on two major areas: use of technology to improve financial inclusion and the protection of wildlife. Beyond his deep engagement with Grameen Foundation since the early 2000s, where he also served as the chair of the board of trustees, Maritz was also an early supporter of the Mifos Initiative, a platform for delivering a complete range of financial services to the poor.[9] The area that has increasingly taken up his energies is the work around conservation and wildlife protection. He owns a wildlife sanctuary in Kafue National Park, protecting a spectacular corner of the world and providing economic opportunities for the local community by supporting and promoting sustainable tourism.

He has also invested in technology solutions by using artificial intelligence and machine vision (imaging-based analysis) to count wildlife via aerial images and camera traps. He's done this because there's a debate about how much wildlife remains. An accurate count allows more accurate quotas for hunting. "I want to introduce real data into these conversations so we can help with these discussions," he says.

Yaffa Maritz, who I interviewed separately, is concentrated on family and child welfare and increasing mindfulness practices in schools. The Maritzes are major supporters of the Center for Child and Family at the University of Washington, where research is being conducted on enhancing the well-being of families and children through the promotion of mindfulness practices.

Paul Maritz warns that "you have to be careful in not falling in love with your particular theory." In this way, he is similar to the Raikeses, and is also open to learning and receiving feedback from other experts. Maritz recommends finding your sweet spot in philanthropy and determining the level of investment you are willing to make as that will determine the scope of what can be done and the organizations with which you'll collaborate.

Emulating the Giving Campaign

During the four and a half years Maritz was the CEO of VMware, starting in 2008, he tried to emulate the Microsoft employee giving program. As VMware did not have the same tradition of giving, Maritz introduced an employee matching gift program and gave people a week's paid leave to spend on any cause of their choice. After their annual sales meeting, all the salespeople would take a day off to volunteer on community projects. "I think it started to raise people's awareness," he says, but he was disappointed that fewer people took the offer of volunteering for a week than he had hoped.

Maritz says philanthropy is not about transforming other people's lives—it's about transforming your own life. "To have that transformation, you have to immerse yourself in real-world experiences," he says. For example, Maritz intellectually understood microlending and supported the Grameen Foundation's work, but he never fully appreciated the power of microlending until he sat through a lending circle meeting in India. "The first one was held at six o'clock in the morning, and it was the most serious business meeting I have been to. These women had children that were dependent upon their making their daily bread—they had no time to waste. [So] this altered my view of things," he says.

Philanthropy is not about shelling out money but about having experiences that alter your worldview. Microsoft's employee giving campaign provides that opportunity for deeper engagement. "For people like me for whom philanthropy was a foreign concept," he says, "it introduced me to organizations like the United Way and the importance of setting aside part of your time and money every year."

Live for Good

Jean-Phillipe Courtois, or JPC, was born in the suburbs of Algiers, Algeria, and moved to Nice in 1962 after Algerian independence from France. JPC's father was a general practitioner doctor who had to restart his life and medical practice after moving to Nice. This was a struggle, as French nationals from the colonies were not welcomed. JPC's extended family network provided vital support that also shaped his value system, which he carries to this day.

JPC finished school and university in Nice, a special place to live given the deep blue waters of the Cote d'Azur and surrounding mountains. "Nice had a mixed population with French citizens returning from the colonies and immigrants from North Africa settling there; it was a city to learn and experiment, and have fun as well," says JPC. He fell in love with computers and microprocessing at the Skema Business School and subsequently interned with a local software company working on developing software for Apple computers.

After graduation, a recruiter approached him to interview for a position at Microsoft in 1984, when Microsoft was still a small company that had been in France for only a year. JPC joined the company as a sales manager and was in charge of recruiting and building the partner ecosystem in France. JPC rode the Microsoft wave and rose rapidly in the ranks: in a couple of years, he was developing the business in Belgium, Greece, the Netherlands, Portugal, and Spain. JPC thrived in this international business environment, taking every opportunity to learn and grow.

Going beyond Selling

JPC became the general manager of Microsoft France in 1994 and ran the subsidiary for four years. It was during this time that he introduced to employees the opportunity to volunteer and become engaged in the community. Employee giving was something new in France—it had a different culture, and employee giving was not an established norm. As a country manager, his job was to run the business, sell and market the products, and be focused on the bottom line. But JPC saw an opportunity for employees to volunteer and support youth by showing them this new world of computers and software, so he launched several initiatives with local nonprofits and national employment agencies where employees would volunteer their time supporting youth. "I did not force anyone," says JPC. Employees volunteered to provide training to kids and introduce them to new skills, such as helping them with their CVs and providing them with training for job interviews. He says, "This was very well received in the community and by our employees, who saw an opportunity to contribute outside of work."

JPC spent two years at the Redmond headquarters under Jeff Raikes, where he developed new tools for measuring customer satisfaction and metrics to evaluate company progress toward its goals, as well as tools for the midyear review process. Upon his return to France in 2000, he became the head of Microsoft Europe, Middle East, and Africa (EMEA). The company was going through a difficult time due to a lawsuit in the United States, new competitors, and a lack of trust among government leaders.

JPC introduced the idea of developing national plans as a way for country managers to work with government officials to align Microsoft's engagement to the top two or three key social issues of interest to that country. As part of the national plans, my team also aligned our philanthropic initiatives, such as teaching technology skills to underserved communities.

One important additional aspect of the national plans was to include some Microsoft partners, especially some small companies, that would work with the local authorities to implement some of the computer skills teaching initiatives. JPC understood the importance of having employees engaged in the community as a way to build trust, align with local priorities, and expand their roots in the community to gain competitive advantage. "This was not a marketing plan created by an agency but a deep-rooted effort driven by the leadership in each country," says JPC.

Artificial Intelligence National Plans

JPC continued his rise in the company, becoming head of Microsoft International, which included every country outside the United States and

Canada. In 2016, CEO Satya Nadella appointed him the head of Microsoft Global, giving him purview over every country. Taking a page from the national plans in 2019, JPC introduced the Artificial Intelligence National Plans to help support the digital innovation in each country where Microsoft had a presence.

"We are connecting the dots between this amazing innovation that is artificial intelligence and people by demystifying this amazing technology that can frighten people, particularly people who do not have the luxury to know or understand the AI tools in their hands and make sense of them," says JPC. His AI framework works on four pillars. The first highlights the digital transformation of the industry by working with key industries that have the biggest share of the GDP. Microsoft works with these companies to effectively utilize AI in their industry. But it also concentrates on their workers and their skill sets and supports the transformation they will need.

The second pillar, AI and Ethics, defines a set of principles Microsoft has created and has shared with governments around the world.[10] The Vatican also joined forces with Microsoft and IBM to promote the ethical development of artificial intelligence, calling for the regulation of intrusive technologies such as facial recognition.[11]

The third pillar, AI Skills, promotes a deeper understanding of AI. For example, Microsoft France is in partnership with a large civic service nonprofit where youth are trained on the basic underpinnings of AI to demystify it. The project is especially focused on a deeper introduction to AI for underprivileged youth in twenty schools around France, with the intention that it will help them enter the workforce. The plan is to expand this effort around the world.

The fourth pillar of this framework is AI for Good, a partnership with nonprofits and social enterprises to create a world of good. JPC becomes very animated when he describes what is already happening. For example, OmniV is a smartphone-based cholera detection system being tested in the field, in Bangladesh and elsewhere. Seabin Project has deployed more than eight hundred trash-skimming devices that have collected more than half a million tons of marine litter, the majority of which is microplastics. Another innovative effort is based in Africa, where Zindi's web platform (more than ten thousand data scientists registered) has hosted dozens of competitions yielding valuable AI solutions for companies, nonprofits, and government organizations across Africa and around the world.[12]

Tragedy Turned to Good

In late 2015, JPC's son, Gabriel, died. A child's death is a massive jolt to any parent. When I spoke to JPC after this tragedy, he was seeking ways to turn it into something positive. Gabriel's web platform, Live for Good, raised funds to build houses in Malaysia. JPC and his family wanted to expand this effort to support creative young people with a desire to be enterprising. JPC, his two daughters, and his wife relaunched the platform as a "Gabriel Live for Good" prize to support action-oriented entrepreneurs who positively want to change the lives of others around the world.

During these past five years, Live for Good[13] has provided 1,500 diverse entrepreneurs in France with training, support, professional coaching, business development, and technology connections. This community of social entrepreneurs is combining the best of positive leadership and social action. One unique aspect is the year-long business-mentor coaching program for entrepreneurs. Another new initiative, Impact Generation, organizes workshops across France to inspire young people to become social entrepreneurs and to drive the movement toward positive social change by providing them with a platform to continue their journey as changemakers.

JPC shared successful graduate stories with me. Cassandra Delage is the founder of Plast'if,[14] a Live for Good laureate in 2017. Her company has developed a machine that transforms single-use plastic into new, useful, and durable 3D-printed objects. These machines are deployed in companies so plastics waste can be collected and transformed into beautiful objects suitable as gifts. In doing so, she has created a movement in France that is transforming consumption patterns and re-creating a circular and caring economy.

Another company, Clear Fashion,[15] has an app launched by Marguerite Dorangeon that allows any individual to choose environmentally and human-friendly clothes. Her goal is to empower citizens to be game changers and make wise consumption choices while supporting brands that have made responsible production choices. These brands work with suppliers who respect labor rights and use processing with low impacts on health and the environment.

Kayoum Fane's platform, Whire,[16] uses AI and machine learning to connect prospective young job seekers to employment by understanding the value of these young people. Through a series of workshops, they help these young job seekers build confidence by using a different approach than traditional employment agencies in France. They focus on using social media and other tools so these young people can market their skills to prospective employers.

From Growth to Purpose Mindset

JPC is one of the most senior executives of one of the largest companies in the world. He is someone who interacts with CEOs of major companies all the time, and I asked him why it is important for businesses to develop the purpose mindset of employees, in addition to the growth mindset. As JPC has grown in his work at Microsoft and Live for Good, his management style has evolved. "I have seen how, by embracing both the growth and purpose mindsets, I am seeing how employees are interacting with customers, how they are positioning their services that the company has to offer, and how that is having a positive impact on the business," he says.

JPC sees the enablement of the growth mindset by ensuring there is a purpose to the company. "It's about building a foundation of values that can help realize the purpose every day by mobilizing the community. It's not a marketing formula that you can come up with in an agency," he says. "It is a destination that gets shaped by your values, the way you work, your principles, the way you support your people and serve your customers, and the community. For me, that has become obvious, but I also get that not everyone gets it."

JPC firmly believes a company cannot succeed without focusing on the success of key stakeholders and developing the purpose mindset of employees to move onto that path. "If, as an organization, you can align with your core purpose and connect the heart and minds of employees," he says, "that becomes extremely powerful."

Bill Sr. and Mary Gates planted the early seeds of purpose at Microsoft, and Bill Neukom nurtured and fertilized the value system within the company through the employee giving and philanthropy program. Successive generations of leaders have continuously evolved these efforts in their own way where it is now getting aligned within the core mission and value system of the company. This evolution from a growth mindset to a purpose mindset is what I hope you will see in the following chapters. Hopefully, it will provide readers with examples of how each one of us and every business can continue to modulate our growth mindset to also embrace purpose in our lives and in our work and in doing so extend the common good.

CHAPTER THREE

The Great Escape

W inner of the 2015 Nobel Prize in Economics, Agnus Deaton is one of the foremost experts on economic development and poverty. In his seminal work *The Great Escape,* Deaton details how the world is a better place than it used to be: "People are healthier, wealthier and live longer."[1] Over the last 250 years, every single human development metric has seen improvement, which is why in the development sector this lifting people out of poverty is called the Great Escape. According to former World Bank Group president Jim Yong Kim, more than eight hundred million people have been lifted out of poverty over the last four decades, with the highest numbers in China and India.[2] When looking at social outcomes concerning poverty, violence, gender rights, health, and education, the world is improving.[3] Modern technological advancements in communication, access to information, health care, and life expectancy have all witnessed great breakthroughs.

Having said this, the Great Escape has been uneven with persistent pockets of inequity and inequality.[4] Furthermore, even if standards of living have improved, the gap between the rich and poor has also increased. In many instances, these inequities and inequalities have been exacerbated by the rapid growth of technology, sometimes creating super-haves and superhave-nots. In *Abundance: The Future Is Better Than You Think*, Peter Diamandis and Steven Kotler discuss the growing inequities because of new technologies such as: artificial intelligence, robotics, 3D printing, internet of things, synthetic biology, and blockchain. They all hold great promise but also create disruption and elicit fears. One way to reduce the inequities is to ensure we have supporting intermediaries—people who will step in to act as bridge builders—those who understand the impact of technology on society and are thinking and acting to bring the benefits of technology and growth to all segments of society.

Deaton also recounts his own Great Escape. His father grew up in a rough coal mining town in South Yorkshire, England. After serving in the army, his father pursued a night-school education, learned surveying skills, and secured a job as an office boy in a civil engineering firm in Edinburgh. In classic fashion, the father ensured that his children would have a better education; through hard work and perseverance, Agnus Deaton graduated from Cambridge and became an economics professor first in the United Kingdom and then at Princeton.

The individuals featured in this chapter have made their own Great Escape. Each has a unique story, though education is a common thread. As the "great equalizer," education allowed them to reach their full potential and build a future for others. They all embrace a purpose mindset to promote the common good. Rather than making their escape and leaving the rest of the world behind, they have enabled others to make their own Great Escape. Rather than focusing on the tragedies of inequities and injustices, these individuals take action and become bridge builders. As Trish Millines Dziko says, "You have it; you share it."

Building a Diversity Pipeline

Trish Millines Dziko has fought against inequality her whole life. She is a Seattle institution, an African American woman working to empower the underrepresented and underserved communities through her Technology

Access Foundation (TAF). In a recent *Seattle Times* article, "A Centennial Celebration of Suffrage: Trish Millines Dziko: 'You have it; you share it,'"[5] she shared her thoughts on inequity and diversity: "'The whole subject of diversity has become a multibillion-dollar industry with very little to show for it,' she says. The tech industry is still primarily male and white. And it's hardly alone. Nonprofits whose constituents are mostly people of color tend to be run by white people. 'They don't look like me, but they're serving people like me.'"

I first met Millines Dziko eighteen years ago. She is a person who exudes joy and purpose. Her work and life's commitment highlight her purpose to ensure that minorities and women have equal access to technology, science, and engineering education.

Millines Dziko was born in 1957. She says her mother, Pat Millines, gave her drive, vision, and selflessness. Millines was single when she adopted Trish, something that was very unusual at the time. Millines cleaned houses for a living but stressed the importance of education and college. Millines Dziko was raised in Belmar, New Jersey. She recalls the town was still segregated when she was growing up, and there were places she could not go as a black girl.

At Asbury Park High School, Millines Dziko was "kind of geeky": she joined the AV club, where she ran the film projector and tape machine; she studied Swahili for three years; and she loved to read. Millines Dziko also showed early math and science aptitude. But because she was black and good at basketball, she was pushed into the "athletic" academic track and assigned to a lower math class. Finally, one teacher recognized her skills in algebra and put her into the math honors track.

From Basketball to Computer Science

She went on to earn a basketball scholarship at Monmouth College, where she majored in computer science. After graduating from college in 1979, Millines Dziko landed a job writing software to test a new military radar system. This job at Computer Sciences Corporation in New Jersey exposed her to both inequities and racism. A woman with a psychology degree and no coding experience earned much more than Millines Dziko. She moved to Hughes Aircraft and here, too, she experienced racism at the hands of her boss who made racist comments. Some coworkers protected her, however, and she did learn new skills and grow. She eventually moved to Fortune Systems before moving to Seattle in 1985 to work as a manager of TeleCalc's testing department.

Millines Dziko was introduced to Microsoft when it was still a small company called the "velvet sweatshop" because of how hard it worked their employees. Millines Dziko moved to Microsoft in 1988 after TeleCalc began layoffs. On top of her regular work, Millines Dziko was frequently asked to take African American recruits out for dinner. She recalls this as being part of "all that extra stuff you do on top of your job because you're tired of being lonely in the company." She became one of the first members of Blacks at Microsoft when it was formed in 1989, which pushed for equal treatment for people of color at the company.

Always seeking to maximize social impact and work toward the common good, Millines Dziko helped transform the giving campaign, even though it was unrelated to her work at the time. When Millines Dziko joined Microsoft, United Way of King County managed the campaign and took 9 percent of donations going to other organizations. Millines Dziko and few others petitioned Microsoft for direct donations, rather than going through United Way. In the interim, they persuaded Microsoft to match to associations like the United Negro College Fund and the Women's Funding Alliance. Microsoft eventually moved to a direct donation system. Millines Dziko explains, "What I liked personally was, when I gave money, watching Microsoft give money right behind me. That really helped a lot of small organizations that I cared about. And it made me feel that I was making an impact." Eventually, she became the senior diversity administrator, working to recruit and retain candidates of color. It was then she decided that increased diversity in the software industry required changing the pipeline.

Diversity in STEM

As part of her job, Millines Dziko ran a high school internship program, which she evolved to also focus on students of color. She recalls when Jill Hull Dziko, who is now Trish's spouse, brought a group of her students from [a middle school in the] Seattle Public Schools to visit Microsoft. She saw the kids' reactions when they saw older kids working on computers. One of the kids said she wanted to be an engineer. That's when Millines Dziko had an epiphany: she realized she could not increase the pipeline from within the confines of Microsoft.

After four months of planning, Millines Dziko turned away from the financial security Microsoft offered and focused on closing the gap between technological haves and have-nots and the implications for children of color. Millines Dziko and her spouse, Hull Dziko, created the Technology Access Foundation, and twenty-three years later, they are still at it. Millines Dziko funded the program herself for the first few years, and then her friends and former colleagues at Microsoft contributed through the giving campaign. The giving campaign also helped them build an expanding volunteer network.

TAF began as an after-school program to introduce students of color to math, science, and computers, as well as to internship opportunities. After they tried to boil the ocean, they eventually focused on a few core programs for high school students and then extended them middle- and elementary-school students. It was not easy. Some years, fundraising was strong, and other years they struggled. As successful as their internship programs were, students still struggled to enter university engineering and computer science majors because they had not taken the right math track in school.

Around 2004, they began to design an experimental school with a tech-focused curriculum within the existing public school system. With some funding from the Bill and Melinda Gates Foundation, they talked to other nonprofits that had started schools. Most had started charter schools. The senior leadership at TAF retooled their organization, hiring people with additional skills to build a school and design the curriculum. Millines Dziko recalls it being a difficult time, as they were designing and launching a new school and at the same time running existing programs.

Their aim was for the new school to be part of the Seattle School District, but that proved difficult. Eventually, they ended up in the Federal Way School District, which is south of Seattle. Opened in 2008, TAF Academy is a sixth-through-twelfth-grade STEM-focused project-based curriculum in a public neighborhood school, designed to prepare students for college and future careers.

According to Millines Dziko, "It took us seven years to get the TAF headquarter building built, and now we own it, and we have no debt, so I am happy." TAF Academy is now on their second ten-year commitment from the Federal Way School District. They have taken this model and are working with other existing public schools to help them transform over a five-year period to operate like the TAF Academy. "Over the course of nine years, we have experienced great success and recognition—both locally and nationally," she says. "We have ridiculously successful numbers, but we also have challenges. And we meet those challenges head-on, and the thing that is hard is the public school system does not turn around fast." As the first school in Washington State to be comanaged by a nonprofit and school district, their students are thriving in a rigorous and relevant learning environment rooted in project-based learning practices for today's college- and career-bound student.

In 2017, with Federal Way Public Schools support, TAF Academy merged with Saghalie Middle School to create TAF@Saghalie and now impacts an additional four hundred students through their STEMbyTAF academic model, ensuring students have the knowledge and experience to use STEM as a tool for positive social change, starting in their own community.

Silicon Valley Mindset

Educational system reform is challenging. Most funders and donors want scalable change, and technology is one key driver to achieving that. Mark Zuckerberg learned the hard way that pouring money—$100 million—on one school district without active community engagement is a recipe for disaster. According to Raj Kumar in *The Business of Changing the World*, tech entrepreneurs like Zuckerberg are often tempted to "parachute in" and try to make fast, sweeping changes, rather than working with community members who are already working on education reform. "Supporting champions in their own communities for prioritizing education and improving the system over time is unappealing," he writes. "It has none of the immediately disruptive characteristics of the technology start-up ethos."[6]

Millines Dziko faces such a dilemma. She says, "There are many schools that were started like ours by somebody in the community. They saw their kids weren't getting the education, so they decided to open a charter school. And they don't want to grow it a whole bunch; they just want to serve their community." The funding community does not support these individuals. Many of these schools close due to lack of funds. Millines Dziko is now using her time and resources from her Pahara Fellowship at the Aspen Institute to study the national education ecosystem and develop ways to enable public education to benefit the students it currently underserves—students of color. She is working with more than five hundred single-site charter schools to raise their profiles and help them secure resources.

Millines Dziko is concerned that, in the pursuit of efficiency and scale, funders forget that education is all about effectiveness. She is also concerned about how technology and personalized learning is replacing people. The important aspect of teaching is moving students from accessing information to gaining knowledge.

As Millines Dziko moves into her next phase, she is trying to find successful models but is also discovering that not all models can be easily replicated across communities. She is concerned about a cookie-cutter approach; her priority is how to be effective in educating students. Millines Dziko is evolutionary, revolutionary, and focused on generational change. Her purpose and her movement are nothing short of changing the world one kid at a time. In her vision, that also means one teacher at a time, one principal, one superintendent, one school board, one PTSA, and one archaic policy at a time. While she's at it, why not try to transform the culture of philanthropy?

Education: The Great Equalizer

Horace Mann, a pioneer of American public schools in the nineteenth century, famously called education the "great equalizer of the conditions of men."[7] The Obama administration's secretary of education, Arne Duncan, has said, "But the inverse is also true. Students who receive a poor education, or who drop out of school before graduating, can end up on the wrong side of a lifelong gap in employment, earnings, even life expectancy."[8]

All over the world, education is seen as a ticket out of poverty, and parents in many parts of the world will invest in their children's education. According to Duncan, "Too often, the difference between a life of promise and a life in peril hinges not on a student's potential but on the quality of the local public school. That means Americans have a choice to make whether we will allow education to be a wedge that widens inequality or whether we will use its power, as Horace Mann envisioned it, to create opportunity for all."[9]

There are thousands of individuals throughout the world who have changed the arc of their life and careers through education. Rajeev Agarwal is one such individual. He grew up in Shahjahanpur, a small town in the Indian state of Uttar Pradesh, one of the most populated and poorest states. Rajeev was the eldest child of a schoolteacher and lawyer but grew up without running water and electricity. He remembers "pumping water and using kerosene lamps to study." He jokes that he escaped television because he did not have electricity. He and his two younger brothers and sister had a happy childhood, and he did not feel deprived. They were lucky to have a two-income household with both parents working; his parents could afford their education.

He studied in the local government-run school, where teachers often did not show up for class. But through his parents' support and his own determination, he excelled: "When I entered the ninth and tenth grades, you know the late teenage years, I realized that I have to get education." His aim was the competitive and elite Indian Institute of Technology (IIT). His parents were unenthusiastic about this risky approach; they believed the eldest son should study at the local engineering college and study for the less-competitive state exam. When Agarwal came across an advertisement in one of the national Indian papers, the *Hindustan Times*, for private preparatory classes for the IIT exam, he told his father he wanted to take them. It was a risky move to send money via a bank draft just to inquire if Agarwal and his current grades would meet the threshold for their program.

Agarwal did enroll, took the IIT exam, passed, and was assigned to IIT Kharagpur (in West Bengal, the same school Google CEO Sundar Pichai graduated from). Agarwal had never heard of the place: "[I] had to go to the train station to find out where Kharagpur was."

At IIT, he joined a cohort of highly westernized students and had to learn how to speak English. After graduating from IIT, he came to the United States and completed his master's of science in engineering at Iowa State. After working for a few years, he completed his MBA at the University of Michigan and was recruited by a campus program to Microsoft in 1993. Agarwal's book *What I Did Not Learn At IIT* shares his life experiences and lessons about becoming a successful business leader.[10]

From a Small Town to a Major Corporation

Agarwal spent seven years at Microsoft, leaving at the height of the dot-com boom to start MAQ Software in early 2000. While at Microsoft, he and his wife, Arpita, also at Microsoft, were involved with the giving campaign. "For the last two to three years of my time at Microsoft, both my wife, Arpita, and I thought we were earning enough and we should take advantage of the matching grant and maximize it," he says. In their early years, they were more focused on paying off student loans and getting settled in a new country. As their income increased, their focus also shifted to investing back into the community from which they came. Given their experiences with education as the great equalizer, with Agarwal's mother being a teacher at a girl's high school, they gravitated toward supporting girl's education. But they also wanted to invest in villages and rural communities.

Their initial investments were to support a local school principal in a village near their hometown and to build a school for girls in a nearby community, but that endeavor took quite a while to get off the ground. They were puzzled as to why girls were not signing up, despite the demand. They discovered that girls ate a free midday meal at government schools. So they introduced a free meal program. Every year, Agarwal and his family spent time in his hometown and visited many of the schools they supported to learn how the students could thrive and learn.

STEM education became their focus. A STEM education provides many opportunities to get a well-paying job, and so they invested in the school where his mother taught. By now, their company was off and running; Agarwal would travel to their office in India to build local connections in the tech industry to help him with this endeavor.

Working with governments is key, especially in the education field. If you want to introduce new programs or opportunities for students, you must get permission from various local bureaucrats, especially if you are not willing to cut corners and grease the wheels. The Agarwals were not going to cut corners, so they turned to his now principal mother to help with the paperwork to launch a STEM program before she retired. Eventually, the school was completed.

Both of the Agarwals have a growth mindset in which they have combined their purpose to improve the quality of education in rural and small-town schools in India. Since that first school, they have supplied science and technology kits to several schools in India. But each time they work with school principals who also have the growth mindset, so they will effectively use their investment and keep their focus on small towns.

In 2000, they started MAQ Software and set up a branch in Mumbai, India. According to Arpita Agarwal, they started training the local kids, especially girls, how to use computers: "Our engineers were using computers during the day, but during evenings the computers were not being used. We said let's put them to use and get local students to come and get lessons on basic Office tools." I visited their offices in Mumbai while I was at Digital Partners and found their approach quite innovative. If most technology firms could create spaces for students to use computers, you could bridge the digital divide. Many years later, I found a similar program in the Philippines where one of the outsourcing firms was working with Microsoft and the Unlimited Potential program to train students from the neighboring community on basic computer skills; many went on to work in their company.

Supporting Systems Change

Over the last few years, the Agarwals have evolved the program they support. They realized that funding one more teacher and one more classroom was not scalable: "With the advances in the internet and mobile, the game is very different now. And we really have to take advantage of the opportunities that technology provides to improve these schools," he says. Their focus shifted to software development as they felt they were uniquely positioned to do this.

In 2014, the Global Learning XPRIZE was announced with funding from Elon Musk to address the challenge of the more than 250 million children around the world who do not have access to learning tools and, even more, who cannot read, write, or do basic math. The Global Learning XPRIZE challenged teams from around the world to develop open-source, scalable learning software that empowers children to teach themselves basic reading, writing, and arithmetic within fifteen months.[11] On May 15, 2019, the XPRIZE announced two grand prize winners: Kitkit School from South Korea and the United States, and onebillion from Kenya and the United Kingdom. The open-source learning programs are available on GitHub with instructions to localize in other languages.

The Agarwals, and their colleagues from MAQ Software, partnered with the XPRIZE to validate some software these teams were working on and to ensure they were fully open source. Since then, they have localized the learning modules in four languages—Indian English, Hindi, Bengali, and Urdu—to reach students in India, Pakistan, and Bangladesh. Improved internet connectivity and availability of power have led to a second program to set up computer labs in the schools they have been working in.

Sixteen labs operate, giving access to at least ten thousand students. They estimate they can scale these labs to reach five hundred thousand students in fifty districts in Uttar Pradesh. They are now developing a blueprint and looking for nonprofit partners who will run these labs and extend their reach. Using the tiny and affordable Raspberry Pi desktop computers with Chrome and other peripherals, they can create a functioning lab for $5,000. Each lab has a teacher and a nurse who can monitor the health care needs of these students, many of whom are anemic and need eye care.

As the Agarwals have matured, so, too, have their programs, moving from interventionist models to more holistic models. They also involve their employees, giving them their own purpose, which only multiplies their impact. According to Agarwal, "Before, I knew them as professionals working on projects or writing software. Now, I can see their personal side, understand what drives them. . . . This is also a growth opportunity for them because they can see how to scale some of these programs in situations where they don't really have absolute control and are learning to use persuasion techniques instead."

Arpita Agarwal has a slightly different take on their combined business and social investment efforts. Their business is the means, and their social investment is the purpose: combining means with purpose provides the most satisfying experience. She also says combined efforts also lead many employees, customers, and other partners to find a common cause. The two efforts combined in collective power can transform the way students learn.

The Agarwals' approach is different from Millines Dziko's. The Agarwals bring their core competency and the deep understating of technology, computers, and IT networks to their new labs. In India, there will never be enough teachers to service the needs of the students; for the Agarwals, technology was an answer to teach skills to the growing youth population and put them on a path toward economic success.

Preparing Future Innovators

In my work at Microsoft, I met with communities, educators, government officials, and business leaders on every continent. Unlimited Potential was one program we offered that taught basic digital skills to members of underserved communities. Over the ten years I was at Microsoft, we supported more than seventy thousand technology learning centers in 102 countries. Many were in remote corners of the world, located in caves in China, in a small desert town in Egypt, in the jungles of Borneo, deep in the Amazon rain forest, or down the street from Microsoft at the local Boys and Girls Club. These learning centers' goals were to expose young people to computers, spark their curiosity, and ignite a new path forward. We also worked with other populations, including the elderly, so they could access government resources or connect with their loved ones in distant locations. In the mid-2000s, we still had only basic internet access and very limited mobile penetration.

Every minister of education or head of state I met wanted to know how we could help them ignite innovators; they wanted to inspire young people to change the world and make their countries competitive in a globalizing world. In 2013, I was invited to speak with the president of Indonesia and to address fifty thousand students and young people who had gathered in a stadium in Jakarta. My job was to inspire them to become entrepreneurs and innovators.

In *Creating Innovators—The Making of Young People Who Will Change the World*, education expert Tony Wanger and documentary filmmaker Robert Compton reveal patterns of what it takes to nurture creativity and spark imagination: a childhood of creative play leads to deep-seated passions, which in adolescence and adulthood blossom into a deeper purpose for career and life goals. The forces that drive young innovators are play, passion, and purpose.

But the process of inspiring innovators is not simple; it takes effort to develop the skills of students to move from rote learning to analytical and creative skills. If given the opportunity, every child can thrive and use their mind.

Implementing a Dream

In 2011, then president of the server and tools division at Microsoft, Satya Nadella, called me. He had just met with Kevin Wang, a young engineer in his division, who was also a high school computer science teacher, and Dave Thompson, a retiring corporate vice president. Thompson had arranged the meeting to share the work he was doing to bring more computer science education programs to schools. Wang had launched a program in 2009 called TEALS (Technology Education and Literacy in Schools) to prepare high school students for the jobs of tomorrow. The program pairs teachers with industry volunteers to teach computer science classes. After ten years, TEALS is now offered in 650 schools in twenty-seven states and Canada. TEALS has taught seventy-five thousand high school students in introductory or AP computer science. In ten years, TEALS has partnered with over a thousand high schools in the US to help build sustainable, successful, and diverse CS programs. Hundreds of teachers teach CS on their own at high schools with established CS programs that TEALS helped build. Why does an electrical engineering and computer science major from the University of California, Berkeley go on to create one of the most sophisticated CS programs in high schools in the United States?

Wang and his parents immigrated to the US in 1989 from Shanghai, China, when he was nine years old. His father sold everything he had and arrived in Los Angeles with a couple of hundred dollars a week before Christmas Eve. Wang and his mother stayed with his aunt in Los Angeles, and his father went on to study electrical engineering at North Dakota State University. His father landed a job in Silicon Valley and catapulted their family into the American middle class, a common experience of immigrants who come to the United States to pursue graduate education.

In high school, Wang taught AVID summer program for rising freshmen, and also fellow students at a high school tutorial center. Though he majored in electrical engineering and computer science at UC Berkeley, his interest in education led him to teaching rather than a tech job or graduate school. He wanted to teach computer science in high school, though there were few schools with computer science classes, even in Silicon Valley. He found a well-off independent school, Woodside Priory, that had a Stanford undergraduate teach computer science occasionally. Wang still shakes his head when he recalls his experience at Woodside, still disbelieving they trusted a twenty-two-year-old to develop a computer science program. After three years at Woodside, he pursued his master's degree in the Technology Innovation and Education program at Harvard.

Wang says wryly, "I had already done the practical stuff and then learned the theory, versus learning the theory and then the practical stuff." He was being recruited for a full-time education consulting career by a prominent education consulting company.

But life chose a different path for Wang. Friends at Harvard asked him to share his resume with recruiters on campus and Microsoft made him an offer. For a kid who grew up on grunge music, Seattle was a draw, so he joined the Office Communicator team to work on adding an education feature in 2006. Kevin was excited to get back to working on engineering and design and being in a technical role.

Computer Science Education in Every High School

In 2009, Wang began to miss education, so he started teaching a computer science class at a local private school. Word soon got around that a Microsoft guy was teaching computer science to high school students, and the Issaquah and Seattle School District foundations approached him through Microsoft to see if he would start a computer science class in their schools. Wang remembers his meeting with the superintendent of the Issaquah School District, who was cautious at taking this meeting but took the meeting at the request of the district's foundation. Once the superintendent discovered Wang had taught high school computer science and had a master's in education from Harvard, his demeanor changed because it is rare to meet an engineer with a formal and practical education background.

The genius of TEALS is that it links industry volunteers with some computer science teaching experience with classroom teachers to teach during the first period. Unlike other education efforts, which aim to disrupt the education and school systems, and often displace or dismiss the importance of the role of the classroom teacher. Wang has a deep understanding of how you can change and evolve teaching from within. By linking teachers with industry volunteers, the expectation is that in a few years the teachers will be able to teach by themselves without the volunteers, allowing the volunteers to go to another school.

After the first two years of TEALS, demand increased, and Wang was at a critical juncture. He wanted to leave Microsoft to start a nonprofit and follow his dreams of having a computer science curriculum in every school in the United States. There are forty-five thousand high schools in the United States, and no more than two thousand have any sort of computer science program. Given industry demand for computer science professionals, not enough computer science graduates will become teachers. When Wang told his manager he was leaving to start a nonprofit, his manager had him speak to Dave Thompson. Thompson was retiring and knew the industry was having difficulty recruiting computer science graduates, especially people from diverse communities. TEALS had created a pipeline of trained high school students who wanted to study computer science and work in the industry. Thompson set up a meeting with his boss, Satya Nadella, with the intention that they might support TEALS and allow Wang to recruit Microsoft employees as volunteer teachers.

Nadella saw the bigger picture and instead suggested that Wang stay at Microsoft and incubate the program within the company, giving Wang a stronger foundation to eventually become a freestanding organization. That is when Nadella called me and asked Community Affairs to house Wang and support the incubation. He provided us with the head count and some seed funding for programmatic costs.

Once Nadella became the CEO, he added more fuel to the TEALS program with an announcement of a $75 million commitment from Microsoft to support computer science education. Code.org (chapter 5) has further popularized the study of computer science and has been given a boost from major IT companies. TEALS has more than nineteen hundred industry volunteers, and 85 percent of them come from companies other than Microsoft. The volunteers have invested more than 1.6 million hours in the classroom, the equivalent of $160 million of time.

TEALS is a demanding volunteer commitment. Volunteers commit two hundred hours a year: summer training and thirty-six weeks of classroom time. For Wang, the monetary value is less important than the time volunteers invest in building bridges between technology and education.

One of my proudest moments was when TEALS expanded into rural schools in 2012, way before other programs focused on rural technical empowerment. They expanded into a school in coal country in eastern Kentucky, one of the poorest counties in the US, via remote video teaching. Today almost 20 percent of TEALS schools are from rural areas in the US (which is the US average). These students have gone on to the University of Pennsylvania and Vanderbilt University and now work in the industry, completely changing the trajectory of their careers and lives. As Wang's father studied in North Dakota, he knew there were needs in rural America: "I was more aware of rural America than I think any other kid who grew up in the Bay Area," Wang says, "and it is the most underserved, so I wanted to be there with TEALS." Today, TEALS is offered in more than a hundred rural schools.

Scaling TEALS

Fifty percent of schools TEALS partners with are Title I schools serving low-income communities. A third of their students are women, which is double the college and tech industry average for computer science. A third are historically marginalized in tech. A majority of students are people of color. In some ways, TEALS reaches more underrepresented students in computer science than some specialty out-of-school computer science programs. TEALS students also score higher than the US average for the AP exam, and a higher percentage enroll in computer science programs in college.

TEALS is an amazing program because Wang brought his computer science and education background to the thorny issue of high school education in this country. He has combined his growth mindset with purpose. He has created something first within the confines of a company working a full-time job but has done so in a way that has attracted hundreds of other companies to join. Many volunteers have joined because of their own background and want to see more diverse people in the industry. For some, it is about inspiring the next generation, and some find great solace in discovering purpose through a subject they are passionate about.

Wang left Microsoft in December 2019 after my interview with him. Wang is now working on his next project focused on reducing computer science education gaps. He was also recently appointed to the WA State Board of Education. For Wang, running the TEALS program has allowed him to help people tap into their deeply personal reasons for finding purpose, and also it helped ensure that the education community was benefited. There is much to learn from the TEALS program, and if volunteers from other industries could also develop similar programs, we can transform the way our children learn.

Empowering Girls and Women

I traveled to the Philippines around Christmas 2007, where I visited Cecilia Flores-Oebanda's Visayan Forum Foundation center (now called Voice of the Free) in Manila and met young girls who had been rescued from their traffickers. Microsoft had given the organization a grant to train these girls. When I arrived just before Christmas with gifts, I was suddenly surrounded by the girls. They tied a pillow to my belly, wrapped a red coat around me, and taped a white beard on my face, just like Santa Claus. I had come bearing gifts, and they wanted to celebrate.

I have never forgotten how the girls lit up as they told me how learning basic computer skills would allow them to find work and earn a small living while they were still in seclusion, as many had court cases pending. Later that evening, I met two other young ladies for dinner. They had been recently rescued from a shipping container by Interpol off the coast of western Africa. These girls were being trafficked to Europe and had been raped multiple times on their journey from the Philippines, taken under the guise of domestic laborers going to work in Europe. They both learned basic computer skills, and one designs letterheads and business cards to earn a living while the other designs websites for restaurants.

During my travels in the Middle East, India, Africa, Latin America, and even Europe and the United States, I heard from many a young girl why education was so key for them to succeed. Soma Somasegar and Akila Somasegar invest their time and money to support girls and women to get educated and have a better life. Soma Somasegar was inspired by his mother, an uneducated housewife who insisted that Soma and his siblings get an education and prioritized her kids' education over everything else. For Akila Somasegar, what inspired her to focus on educating and empowering girls was experiencing in India the death of her maid's daughter at age seventeen due to childbirth complications.

Embracing Opportunities

Soma Somasegar joined Microsoft in 1989. Born in Pondicherry, a small town in southern India, his family struggled to make ends meet. But since his parents prioritized education, Soma was able to graduate from an engineering college in Chennai in southern India. And he realized his goal of receiving graduate education in the United States through a scholarship.

Akila Somasegar was also born in southern India, and her father was a government officer. He, too, had escaped poverty through education, so he ensured that his daughter was educated.

I interviewed them on a sunny summer afternoon at their plush home in Medina, a tony neighborhood in Seattle where Bill Gates and other Microsoft alumni reside. Akila looks back and says she constantly remembers the days she played with Lakshmi (the maid's daughter, who did not have an opportunity to go to school); if she had not married at fifteen, she might be alive today and might have lived a better life had she received an education. Akila's circumstances were different, as she did get an education and was able to join Microsoft in 1994 when she married Soma. She worked in the finance group on the international team and was the point person for Africa, India, and the Middle East. She enjoyed being part of a global community at Microsoft and loved the people she worked with. When her daughters were born, she left Microsoft to raise her family, given the unsustainable hours she was working. She wanted to go back to Microsoft after the kids were older but ended up working for a start-up that eventually got acquired. At that same time, she was invited to join the advisory board of the United Nations Foundation's Girl Up program working on girl's empowerment programs with several UN agencies, including with UN Population Fund on stopping child marriage in India.

At the same time, Soma's career at Microsoft was accelerating, and he soon managed the entire developer group. I asked him about his engagement in the employee giving campaign. He was frank, saying he participated but was never deeply engaged. His work was his first, second, and third priority. He gives credit to Bill Gates for having a much larger vision to build a company where everybody gets to share the wealth. The employee giving campaign is the extension of the principle that everybody in the Microsoft community is going to benefit, not just a handful of people. Somasegar reiterated what Bill Neukom saw in these young, hard-working, talented, and driven individuals—they were determined to make Seattle a place to live and grow and invest back into the community. For them, investing both within their community and outside is a principle they have lived by.

Cochairing the Employee Giving Campaign

In 2008, I asked Somasegar to become the cochair of the employee giving campaign. He was extremely hesitant, as the Somasegars have been private about their philanthropy and community investments; he felt more comfortable asking people to consider as opposed to asking to contribute. But after a couple of conversations, he agreed if we were willing to set a goal of $100 million. The year before, we had raised $90 million, so this was a stretch goal, especially as we were entering a recession and moving away from having big goals to reduce the competitive nature of the employee giving campaign. Nevertheless, Pamela Passman and I reluctantly agreed. For Somasegar, setting an aspirational goal was key to exciting his growth mindset. He felt it also key to aligning with a purpose that in hard times we must do more.

In the twenty years he had been with the company, he was aware of how aligned the employee giving campaign was with the values of the company, and the company and its employees played a meaningful role in giving back to the community. For Somasegar, leading the overall giving campaign was an honor and a privilege. Under his leadership, we met the $100 million goal. Somasegar understood that having such a large goal was an opportunity to excite thousands of employees to get engaged. He says, "When you see it across the whole company, literally like thousands of people coming together, it is like, oh my god, that is something magical that's happening."

Focus: Hyperlocal, Regional, and Global

Akila Somasegar serves on the boards of the YWCA, which focuses on eliminating racism and empowering women, and Bellevue Life Spring, which is a hyperlocal organization in Bellevue supporting kids in the local school and people in need. Joining the board of the YWCA was like coming back full circle as the Somasegars had cooked meals for the last twenty years at Angeline Shelter, a YWCA program. As a newly married couple and new to Seattle, they, with some of their friends, decided to cook meals for a local shelter with the goal of giving back a little to the community.

Soma piped in to say, "Our work extends out in concentric circles from the hyperlocal to the regional to the global." At the same time, their work also extends out in circles from supporting basic immediate needs, like serving meals, to supporting training programs that provide an economic foundation and raise girls and women out of poverty.

Akila's work in Rajasthan State in India, through Girl Up, UNF, helps educate girls so they do not end up in child marriages. Girls as young as eight years old are often getting married. She works with local organizations and community workers who provide training and support to these girls so that they stay in school. They are also very careful to ensure that they bring along the elders to try and overcome the old traditions and customs of child marriage.

Akila shares a story of her visit to Sri Lanka, an experience that motivates them in their work of creating economic opportunities for girls and women. As part of her work with the UN Foundation, she was in Sri Lanka to launch Girl Up nationwide. While she was doing the launch, she also got involved in supporting economic empowerment programs in the northern part of the country, which had been engulfed in a separatist war led by the Tamil Tigers. Many women are widows and sole providers for their families. Many have leased small plots of land to grow food but have no skills, and they are unable to keep up with the market because the cost of production is high. They then are forced to take out loans they cannot pay back, trapping them in further poverty and creating a vicious, inescapable cycle. Akila did the Girl Up launch working with the Ministry of Children's Welfare and Ministry of Education, they started a program to empower these women economically. After the launch, Akila visited some of the war widows in the former war zone. She met a sixty-five-year-old woman who earned a living making handmade greeting cards. She had employed three other people; during the visit, the woman asked Akila to buy her a computer and a printer. She wanted to use the computer to design better cards, become more efficient, and increase her business.

Akila asked her if she knew how to use a computer, and the woman told her that when she had heard people were coming to help them, she had enrolled in a computer class in the next village so she would be prepared to ask for the computer. She walks three miles every day to get to the village for her training and at the same time keeps her business going. This woman had no idea that Akila would come and visit her house, but she took a chance and was prepared. Economic empowerment is a major incentive to help people out of poverty. The Somasegars use the combined power of social and economic empowerment in their work. They want to make sure they are effectively using their growth and purpose mindsets to create a virtuous cycle to empower the community.

Today, Soma Somasegar is the managing director at Madrona Venture Group, a venture capital firm based in Seattle. At Madrona, he uses his experience and knowledge to help the next generation of entrepreneurs set up companies and scale them to be successful. He also ensures that there is an overarching purpose to the work of these entrepreneurs, helping them, in their own way, to find a balance between growth and purpose.

Akila is very excited to serve on the Global Leadership Council for the United Nations Foundation. The Council members are invited by the United Nations Foundation's executive office to play a leadership role in bolstering America's relationship with the United Nations. "In today's day and age, where the US administration is cutting back on UN programs such as WHO, it is critical that we continue to advocate for the United States strong support of the United Nations.

Millines Dziko, the Agarwals, Wang, and the Somasegars have taken their experience from Microsoft—a hypercompetitive environment—and applied some of those same principles of the growth mindset to create opportunities for others' Great Escape.

CHAPTER FOUR

Extending the Common Good

The shift from the "greatest generation" to the "me generation" in the United States was captured in Robert Ringer's 1977 *New York Times* bestseller, *Looking Out for #1*. The book extolled the virtues of selfishness to a broad and enthusiastic audience, says former secretary of labor Robert Reich. Millions of people have bought into Ringer's philosophy of winning at all costs. His mantras of "individualism, self-responsibility, personal freedom, and above all the idea that people are above government" all sound reasonable. This focus on individualism and selfishness, however, has created a loss of connectedness, especially in our civic life.

Not everything we do as individuals is selfish—we are still generous, kind, and give back to our communities. Many of us volunteer, while others pitch in during disasters, as I have shown. As a society, we have also become more inclusive, with improvements in rights for minority communities and the general well-being of society.

In *The Common Good*, Robert Reich confronts this trend toward selfishness by making a powerful argument for returning to the promotion of the "common good." He writes that societies "undergo virtuous cycles that reinforce the common good as well as vicious cycles that undermine it, one of which America has been experiencing for the past five decades and must be reversed." To recover this common good, we need to rediscover our citizenship obligations and our responsibilities for communities.[1]

Restoration of the "common good" is an approach to reinstate the purpose of society—an all-encompassing concept that allows each of us to think about our own individual trajectory and impact but also to consider how the interaction between the personal and collective can lead to a better society. In the following vignettes, I show how several Microsoft alumni have tried to re-create the common good as they bring their Microsoft experiences to bear in their current work. Unlike many other alumni featured in this book, these alumni's impact has been to influence people in their social circles not only to become involved in the common good but to take it on as their own cause—to develop their own purpose mindset. Rather than focusing on recruiting volunteers and gathering resources for direct service community work, their work is to transform philanthropists themselves—so that they, too, will extend the common good. By doing so, they are transforming the very nature of philanthropy. These alumni all joined or created organizations that went beyond extending their own values to developing models that not only impact the larger society but can also be emulated in other parts of the world.

Extending Justice and Racial Equity

Anderson H. Brown was born in 1880, in Charleston, West Virginia. His parents, Henry and Margaret Brown, had been slaves. For his granddaughter Andrea L. Taylor, who recently served the president and CEO of the Birmingham Civil Rights Institute, he represents a model of how to live life and interact with others. Brown, who lived to age ninety-four, became an entrepreneur and invested in real estate, owning several properties, even though he did not have formal education beyond the fourth grade. He insisted his children should go to college. Taylor's mother,

Della, earned her Masters degree from Boston University in 1945 and her brother Willard Brown earned his LLB and Masters degree in Law also form Boston University in 1935 and 1937, because they could not attend graduate school in West Virginia as a person of color; the state, however, did subsidize their higher education out of state.

Andrea Taylor was born in 1947 and grew up in Cambridge, Massachusetts, where both her parents studied; her father, Francis C. Taylor earned a Masters degree in violin also from Boston University. Growing up in this multiracial, integrated community was her benchmark as she moved forward in her life's journey. She was uprooted abruptly from this integrated environment when her family moved back to Charleston, West Virginia, in 1956.

Taylor recalls her grandfather's stories about growing up as a child of slaves and about life in general for African Americans during the late nineteenth century. He also told her about tracing her lineage to Ghana in West Africa. Brown was an active member of the community and the deacon of his church, which he helped construct. His name is still engraved on the cornerstone of that church. Taylor's parents returned to their home state after graduate school, and so did Uncle Willard, applying their skills to help improve their community. Uncle Willard headed the local chapter of the NAACP and organized the West Virginia delegation to the March on Washington for Jobs and Freedom. Her uncle and grandfather were at the forefront of lawsuits in West Virginia to open public accommodations and facilities to people of color.

The March on Washington

As a teenager, Taylor accompanied her uncle and mother to Washington, DC, to participate in the historic march organized by Martin Luther King Jr. and his colleagues. The August 28, 1963, march was intended to bring attention to the injustices faced by people of color. People from all over the nation traveled to Washington to demonstrate for jobs and freedom. Taylor recalls the anxiety she had on the bus ride from West Virginia to Washington, DC. All the young folks there knew they were part of something momentous. "There was just a sea of humanity," she says. "I mean, there were tens of thousands of people also arriving in buses, in similar circumstances as our own." Though it was a hot day, a sense of community had formed, even before the march, as they prepared to make a statement to the nation. Despite much anxiety, people had calm and polite interactions—in the midst of this gathering, those there realized that 250,000 people from across the nation were eyewitness to a movement. "It was an exhilarating experience to listen to the 'I Have a Dream Speech'; at that moment, even the youngest among us knew that history had just happened there that day and something transformational had taken place, and it gave shape and direction to my work," Taylor says.

As I interviewed Andrea Taylor, she became wistful: "In many ways, we're still working on achieving aspects of that dream well into the twenty-first century." As she looked out her office window in Birmingham, Alabama, she had a direct view of the 16th Street Baptist Church where four young girls were killed in a violent act of domestic terrorism on September 15, 1963, only eighteen days after the March on Washington. "Today, we still find many barriers to opportunity, and there are many injustices and inequity in our communities with still record levels of poverty," she says. "People don't have access to housing and jobs and health care, and the like. And there's almost a direct line between that experience and recognition and the work that I did recently in Alabama." Being at the helm of the Birmingham Civil Rights Institute for nearly five years, Taylor believes she was at the right place at the right time, using skills she has honed over decades to make a modest contribution to the quest of racial justice and equity, thereby extending the common good.

Moving into Organized Philanthropy

Taylor graduated from Boston University with a degree in journalism in 1968 and started her career as a journalist working as a reporter, producer, and on-air host for the *Boston Globe* and WGBH TV in Boston. After a few years, she moved to Cleveland, where she focused on raising her family of two boys and a daughter. She continued to be active in the community, participating in her kids' school and getting engaged in the local philanthropic organizations, including the YWCA.

Taylor's engagement was getting noticed, so she was invited to join the board of the Cleveland Foundation, the nation's first and one of the largest community foundations in the country. This was her introduction to organized philanthropy. The Cleveland Foundation was established in 1914 by banker Fredrick Harris Goff, who created a dynamic approach to engaging members of the community to help solve community problems. He harnessed the desire of people to help one another by sharing resources for the common good.[2] By serving on the board, Taylor was exposed to the national philanthropic community, attending several conferences and other events around the country. She was introduced to the Ford Foundation, one of the largest philanthropic organizations at that time. The Ford Foundation was interested in learning better ways to grow local philanthropic efforts. They launched an initiative to strengthen local community foundations and to provide them with incentives to grow and become more strategic about how they allocated their resources.

Taylor was hired as a consultant to travel the county and assess, evaluate, and help articulate a program for enhancing these community foundations. During one of her visits, she met a young film producer, Henry Hampton, who had produced an extraordinary documentary series called *Eyes on the Prize*. This fourteen-hour public television series tells the story of the civil rights movement: what led up to the movement, what the movement was about, and the ordinary people who made it happen. These extraordinary ordinary people offered their personal testimonies, which were supplemented by newsreel and archival footage. The series was divided into two segments, and the first segment had been completed. The Ford Foundation had provided support for the first segment and were assessing whether they should continue support.

After Taylor met with Henry Hampton and his team, she returned to the Ford Foundation and suggested to them that "they should not walk but run with as much support as they could muster to help this project go forward to completion." As a journalism major, she recognized the uniqueness ordinary people's voices represented, especially those voices that were part of an extraordinary force for social change in this country.

She says, "This was a powerful narrative about social change and a desire to turn back injustices that were being visited on our communities."

The Ford Foundation took her advice and not only continued their support for *Eyes on the Prize* but also saw the value in promoting people's voices and enhancing authentic storytelling through media, film, television, and radio. They hired Taylor in 1988 to set up the New Media Fund, which she directed for a decade. The late 1980s and early 1990s was a time of global transition: perestroika and glasnost in the Soviet Union, the Berlin Wall coming down, the end of apartheid in South Africa, and changes in military governments and dictators in Latin America. Taylor traveled the world and documented many of these transitions through storytellers all over the planet, particularly those addressing the needs of poverty and social injustice. She also had a front-row seat observing the evolution of social media, witnessing the beginning of two decades of unprecedented digital change.

Every Employee a Philanthropist

I hired Taylor in early 2006 to lead the North America team. Her reputation was stellar, and she had deep community connections, which is what we needed to expand our US programs. Taylor was just finishing up a project at the Educational Development Center, where she had established the center for media and community supported by the Benton Foundation. Taylor saw working at a corporation as a way to complete her experience, having worked at a major foundation and having helped to set up a program at a large nonprofit. Microsoft's philanthropic program had matured, the employee giving program was growing, and we were entering a new program expansion phase.

What convinced Taylor to join Microsoft was the company's early adoption of and commitment to a culture of philanthropy. She saw it as a privilege to work alongside smart, innovative, and committed people who wanted to improve their reach and impact. I asked her to reflect on her experience with the giving campaign after five years of being away from Microsoft: "The employee giving campaign is just wonderful, and I do not think there is anything quite like it. What is unique is that as Microsoft created wealth for its employees, it also provided them an opportunity to become strategic in how they invested and shared that wealth. So the idea that you could have a company where not only is the CEO, founder, and chairman a philanthropist working on a world stage, but there's a program that allows every single employee to be a philanthropist." For Taylor, Microsoft's employee engagement program is an example where highly skilled and highly trained people are encouraged to bring their tools and resources to communities and seek to solve problems for the common good in a purposeful way. It also helps employees refine their own sense of purpose and see themselves as a positive force in society.

At Microsoft, Taylor led support for national organizations bridging the equity divide: the Boys and Girls Club of America, Year Up, and the Network for Teaching Entrepreneurship. She was also instrumental in persuading Microsoft to support the National Museum of African American History and Culture in Washington, DC, thereby leaving an indelible mark through her work.

As part of Martin Luther King Jr. Day celebrations in 2007, Taylor was invited by Blacks at Microsoft to view the showing of the documentary on the March on Washington. As a few thousand employees sat in the audience, Taylor pointed at the screen, showing her colleagues where she had been sitting that day with her high school sweetheart. Other people heard her, and suddenly a murmur rippled through the auditorium that someone who had participated at the march was in the audience. In a company full of young people, Taylor felt like a dinosaur—someone coming to life from a museum of natural history. But Taylor was the elder that had brought with her the full experience of life and was leading the effort to build the purpose-driven culture for Microsoft.

Coming Full Circle

In 2014, Taylor joined the Faith and Politics pilgrimage, reenacting the 1965 march from Selma to Montgomery led by Representatives John Lewis and Steny Hoyer. Taylor was excited to once again get to meet

Congressmen Lewis up close and personal, whom she had remembered hearing at the March on Washington in 1963; Lewis was one of the youngest speakers there. The pilgrimage included a visit to the Birmingham Civil Rights Institute, the first time Taylor had been there. Though the visit lasted only an hour due to a tornado watch, Taylor was reminded of her Ford Foundation work: the institute documented the heroic work of ordinary people and gave voice to their cause.

In her interview with me, sitting at the institute, Taylor felt she had come full circle in her life's journey. It began with the slave ships that brought her great-grandparents to America and continued with the struggle to overcome racial hatred and injustice. It was as if her whole life's work had prepared her for that moment and her new role. She has pulled together her rich collective experiences to take the civil rights narrative to the next level. This became even more apparent when she joined the 2016 opening ceremonies of the National Museum of African American History and Culture, an effort she had championed at Microsoft.

Given the fractured times we live in, Taylor feels her work today helps people focus on the common good: "This is what makes me excited to wake up in the morning every single day for all my professional life, that there is this overlay between personal values and values that have a broader community purpose mindset."

Shifting the Arrogance of Philanthropy

The Atlanta Project (TAP) was launched by former president Jimmy Carter and the Carter Center in 1992 to motivate disadvantaged families to take charge of their well-being with the active involvement and support of the community. Civic and religious leaders, community residents, and corporate executives were spending their time in the community applying their skills to address some of the most vexing problems facing inner cities in the United States. In 1995, I met Linden Longino, a vice president of SunTrust Bank who was working at one of the local schools in inner-city Atlanta to help solve one of the toughest challenges of improving the quality of education. He was on a steep learning curve, having come from a corner office to a school in disrepair. As a privileged white male working with primarily black folks, he knew he had to leave behind his corporate arrogance and learn to listen and work with community leaders, educators, teachers, and parents so they could address the deep challenges facing these communities. The Carter Center did not go in to fix a problem but engaged with the community and empowered them with critical support to address their own challenges.[3]

I was reminded of my visit to Atlanta and the work of TAP when I interviewed Paul Shoemaker. Shoemaker is the former CEO of Social Venture Partners, an organization that has incorporated some TAP approaches to encourage donors to work in partnership with the community to address complex societal issues. Shoemaker joined Microsoft in 1991 after working at Nestle for five years. Like so many others profiled in this book, Shoemaker was struck by how smart people were at Microsoft and how much he had to learn. "The first year at Microsoft was insanely hard," he says. "It was being thrust into major league baseball and facing a fastball from Roger Clemons . . . what doesn't kill you makes you stronger."

One aspect of Microsoft he really enjoyed was the company's rapid growth, moving from a few thousand employees to several thousand employees. Along with that growth also came the launch of several successful products, such as Windows 3.1 and Windows 95. He was excited to be surrounded by high achievers and learn how to work with folks, some of whom were arrogant. He learned, however, how to peek behind that mask—a lesson that would prove valuable later when he worked with Social Venture Partners. He, like some of the others in this book, observed the employee giving campaign from the sidelines—participating but not fully engaged. He also felt that, early on, many employees did not know about the great matching program. He thought many employees were just focused on keeping their heads down, shipping products, and not looking to get engaged in the community. He says, "My brother works at the post office, and he works just as hard, so working hard was not unique to Microsoft." But as the company matured, Microsoft encouraged its employees to be engaged with the community in an authentic way: "I can actually ship Windows 95 and still do some good."

Shoemaker's three major lessons from Microsoft are: learning how to play in the big leagues and survive; learning how to overcome setbacks and keep going; and learning from smart and effective people. But he also realized that in such an environment one could become cocky and arrogant, so he watched himself. "I am not Mr. Humble, I think, but I am not arrogant."

In 1994, Shoemaker met with Barbara Dingfield, director of Community Affairs, who laid the pathway for Shoemaker's future work in the community. He grew up in Iowa, son of a Methodist minister and a mom who was involved in the community, so he had early experience of being involved. Therefore, when Shoemaker decided to poke his head up from his work, Dingfield guided him to join the board of the Seattle Children's Alliance.[4] Shoemaker had enough humility to observe and learn from the other board members and understand where he could add value during his first year. He reminded me that in the midnineties most folks volunteered as tutors, participated in neighborhood cleanup activities, or coached their kids' little league games. Applying your professional skills was not central to most employee volunteering programs.

Adding Value through Acumen

Through listening and observing, Shoemaker realized how to add value. He was surrounded by experts who had tremendous content experience and could go deep, but he could offer a more horizontal perspective about organizational leadership and strategy, and about measuring results in mission-driven organizations. Shoemaker gained enormous experience serving with the Children's Alliance. In late 1997, Shoemaker considered his next move while visiting family. He shared that he was looking to leave Microsoft. His dad—the Methodist minister—said, "What the hell is wrong with you?" But Shoemaker was financially stable enough to make the choice: "I made more money than I deserved, but I was not independently wealthy."

In early 1998, he attended the launch of Social Venture Partners, a new model for collective giving. The event featured accomplished Seattle luminaries such as Bill Neukom, Ida Cole, Scott Oki, and Doug and Maggie Walker, as well as Paul Brainerd, cofounder of Aldus, the desktop publishing software company. Intrigued by this idea of bringing people together to collectively invest in the community—betting on people and their acumen—Shoemaker met with Brainerd, who offered him the job to run this new organization.

Shoemaker served as the executive director of Social Venture Partners, Seattle, for seventeen years, helping to put the organization on the global map. He worked with SVP partners to engage with the philanthropic community to shift their mindsets from arrogance—something that has plagued the philanthropic world—to humility. The fundamental premise of SVP, Shoemaker says, was to help budding philanthropists "not only to invest their money but to use their brains, and dirty their shoes." SVP committed their financial capital but also their social capital. Not only were grants made to nonprofits in the community, but SVP partners would spend time with these nonprofits, bringing their skills and expertise to these resource-constrained organizations. Shoemaker says, "We're trying to build stronger nonprofits and also trying to build stronger civic and philanthropic leaders."

Similar to Linden Longino's experience in Atlanta, SVP partners discovered how communities in South King County lived and the challenges they faced. The partners met in the nonprofits' dilapidated offices that had no internet connection; these organizations were tackling difficult problems with minimal resources. This "dirtying the shoes" exposed these budding philanthropists to the reality from which they had thus far been removed.

"That was an awesome education," said Shoemaker. Partners were helping strengthen these organizations, but through the process of continuous community engagement, the relationship dynamics slowly shifted: many of these individuals learned how to bring their skills in a way that mattered and was not disruptive for the sake of disruption. Many early SVP partners were from the tech industry, where they prided themselves on disruption and being a disruptor: Will Poole and Tony Mestres (featured later in this chapter), as well as Ravi Venkatesan (chapter 5), have all been SVP partners. By giving SVP partners deep exposure to the community, as President Carter did in the Atlanta Project, these individuals shifted from focusing on their own growth mindset to a purpose mindset through learning how to work and partner effectively with mission-driven organizations.

A Builder, Not a Creator

Shoemaker was not the brains behind the SVP model: "I am not the creative, vision type. I am good at taking Lego pieces and building something out of them." Joining SVP was serendipitous; it was not normal in the midnineties for philanthropists to sit down with their nonprofit partners to determine where and how investments should be made. New Profit in Boston, the Roberts Fund in San Francisco, and Venture Philanthropy Partners in DC were some of the organizations that were going beyond writing checks. Individuals in these groups actively invested their time and, in addition to helping nonprofits with their programs, would focus on strengthening their capacity. Today, this is a much more accepted approach, but twenty years ago, Shoemaker and the founders were not sure this nascent model would work.

It turned out Shoemaker was at the right time and place to help lead this organization. "Having a peer community and an internal peer group and knowing where your money was going was something visceral, and people wanted to be part of that approach," he says. The model is now succeeding not just in the United States, but in Australia, Canada, China, India, Japan, and South Korea. One of the reasons Ravi Venkatesan joined SVP and launched the India chapter was that many people in India did not trust nonprofits because of a lack of transparency. The SVP model overcomes that barrier: SVP partners could direct how their money was spent and could observe its impact.

The initial growth of SVP was organic to some extent. People read about SVP in airline in-flight magazines (these were days before the internet) or saw or read about it in the local news. The initial vision for the Seattle chapter in 1998 was to grow by involving the budding philanthropists from Microsoft and the tech sector. But people started calling from other cities. Over the next few years, SVP grew to five or six other cities. This prompted SVP leadership to grow more deliberately by creating a federation model like Planned Parenthood and the Boys and Girls Club. It was clear to Shoemaker and his team that the SVP model would succeed only if there was local ownership, with headquarters providing support but not leading the way.

Using Social Capital

The key to SVP's success and Shoemaker's ability to make it part of a movement was not resting on organic growth. Paul was deliberate in turning organic interest in SVP into an intentional effort to grow the organization. "I had social capital . . . and I was walking around the country utilizing it," he says. Everyone has social capital, but becoming intentional about using this capital effectively is something we can all learn to do. Shoemaker collected business cards from every conference he attended and would enter them into a database, write follow-up notes, and then continue to follow up. During every visit to prospective cities, he made sure to meet with a range of people and determine how serious they were about starting an SVP chapter. His approach was intentional. "Organic growth quickly turns into chaos if not guided by some intentionality," he says.

Through his training at Microsoft, Shoemaker developed an instinctual feel for determining the right groups to partner with—he could talk to twenty people in any given city and figure out if they were the right partners. He had to determine if a philanthropist was interested in SVP just because they wanted support for their own charity or if they had a genuine desire to become part of the collective giving movement.

He also had to be careful, however, as he met with some well-known individuals, many wealthy and powerful. He had to sharpen his acumen in dealing with them without offending anyone. "Fundamentally, philanthropy is one of the most arrogant acts," he says. In *Winners Take All: The Elite Charade of Changing the World*, Anand Giridharadas questions why rich elites constantly rebrand themselves as saviors of the poor, continually doing more good, but don't focus on doing less harm. For Shoemaker, it was important to make sure future SVP partners understood this new, more highly engaged model of collective giving, which included their time, their talent, and their treasure.

In his seventeen years at SVP Seattle, and as the founding president of SVP International, Shoemaker led the growth of the organization to forty-plus affiliates in eight countries. SVP and SVPI have connected more than thirty-four hundred partners with nonprofits and social enterprises and together have invested more than $70 million in nine hundred nonprofits. Paul is the author of *Can't Not Do: The Compelling Social Drive That Changes Our World* and is focused on working with individuals and organizations to become effective philanthropists. Shoemaker ended our interview by saying, "It's very hard to solve social problems. The private sector has two clear outcomes—making more money than you spend and having customers who buy your product. If you do these two things, then for the most part you succeed. The social sector, on the other hand, does not have these clear market signals, so we invent all of these convoluted processes that, in fact, get in the way of making progress." He hopes that, through his work at SVP and his book, he will inspire a new generation of philanthropists to become deeply engaged and get their shoes dirty. He is concerned with the current state of affairs in the world, where we have retreated into our respective silos. Shoemaker believes that unless we as leaders lead from the middle, we will see limited progress on the major issues facing humankind. He hopes to utilize his skills of leading from the middle to continue working on social challenges: "I cannot sit on the sidelines."

Venture Philanthropy to Impact Investing

Philanthropy means the love of humanity; a conventional modern definition is "private initiatives for the public good, contrasting it with business endeavors, which are private initiatives for private good, and public initiatives which are for the public good."[5] Andrew Carnegie and John D. Rockefeller were the strongest proponents of institutionalized philanthropy, with Carnegie establishing the Carnegie Corporation of New York in 1911 with a $25 million endowment and Rockefeller establishing his foundation in 1913. For the next sixty years, thousands of philanthropic institutions were established by the wealthy to address the root causes of societal problems.

The term *venture philanthropy* was introduced by John D. Rockefeller III in 1969 to describe an imaginative and risk-taking approach to philanthropy that may be undertaken by charitable organizations.[6] This was a very interesting evolution in the thinking and operating of social-purpose organizations. In the early- to mid-nineties, several organizations like Social Venture Partners were developing an engaged model of social impact. This was also the time when companies at the forefront of computing where getting established, and there was a new generation of wealth being created. Will Poole was introduced to philanthropy during that time.

Poole began his professional career at the dawn of the personal computing era. Having graduated with a degree in computer science, he was fortunate to have sold a company and made a little bit of money and ended up working for another early technology innovator—Sun Microsystems—learning the ropes within a corporate environment. The entrepreneur bug bit him again, and he moved to the Bay Area and launched eShop, a pioneering e-commerce platform. They were fortunate enough to be discovered by Microsoft, which was playing catch-up in the rising wave of e-commerce, and moved to Seattle. Poole and his wife, Janet Levinger, had little disposable income early in their career and often maxed out on credit cards. He was in the start-up world, taking a big risk on their future. They were also engaged in a casual, small way in personal giving. That all changed when Microsoft acquired eShop, and suddenly they moved from being in debt with a start-up to having reasonable assets and an incredible future. Their introduction into the world of philanthropy was happenstance. Poole and Levinger were becoming more engaged in the community and looking for opportunities where they could connect and meet like-minded individuals. Janet saw an ad in the local newspaper about a group of people that were starting Social Venture Partners and went to the same opening meeting that Paul Shoemaker attended in early 1988. They, too, were inspired by the vison and idea put forth around collective giving. With an initial contribution of $5,000, they became SVP partners.

The venture philanthropy approach resonated with Poole, having started his journey with support from venture capitalists. He was interested in applying the same principles to social issues: "You could get involved beyond just writing checks to applying talent and acumen as business leaders, and that could be even more valuable." He clarified that check writing is important, and in some cases that's what's needed most, but the idea of SVP was consistent with the way he had been involved in venture capital.

Growing and Developing Emerging Markets

In the early 2000s, Will Poole led the Windows Client division, a product that had a high market share and incredibly strong profits. Windows was selling well in the developed markets, but room for growth was getting narrower; in emerging markets, where they had virtually no consumer share, there were opportunities. Microsoft was selling to some large companies and governments. But there was no connection to middle- or low-income populations. Poole created a group in his division to focus on understanding what was happening in these high-growth segments of emerging markets, economies Microsoft had left unexplored. Through that effort, Poole gained a deep and visceral understanding of the impact of the "digital divide": "There was a large segment of the world that had no access to the world of technology and access to information that the internet represents."

To build a business for Microsoft in emerging markets, Poole's team had to develop scenarios of how consumers in mid- and lower-tier emerging markets would use and benefit from personal computing and from access to information. This became his next calling in life: "How do you apply the development of products and services, and business and financial opportunities, in emerging markets in such a way to make both money and make a difference at scale?"

Poole, along with Orlando Ayala, former group vice president of sales, pitched the idea of creating a new business unit within Microsoft, which led to the creation of the Unlimited Potential Group (UPG). This group brought together several different products from other groups, and by applying new business strategies, they were able to offer these products to consumers in the emerging markets. UPG became a great test site for

Poole to take the company's resources and products and learn about applying global business principles, as well as understanding scale, innovation, and technology: to do some good and make some money.

Going Far Together

Paul Brainerd said to Poole many a time: "It is not what you do in life that matters as much as what you can convince other people to do." This is similar to the proverb "If you want to go fast, go alone. If you want to go far, go together." When Poole left Microsoft and became deeply engaged with SVP, he helped create a program in Seattle called SVP Fast Pitch, which he imported from SVP Los Angeles. He rallied SVP members and others to mentor entrepreneurs in the Seattle ecosystem by helping them prepare an effective business pitch in front of a thousand people. I was an early supporter of this effort from the Microsoft end, especially encouraging Poole and SVP to create a focus on social entrepreneurs, so they, too, could have the same opportunity.

SVP Fast Pitch was gratifying to Poole as hundreds of people in Seattle became mentors. At the same time, Will was exploring new opportunities and was traveling to India quite frequently. He would regularly meet Ravi Venkatesan there, whom he had known quite well because Venkatesan was the chairman of Microsoft India. They would frequently discuss challenges in India, especially environmental and social challenges, and what could be done. Will discovered that high–net worth individuals in India were uniquely jaded. The government did not accomplish much, and nonprofits were, for the most part, unaccountable and porous. Therefore, many of these newly minted high–net worth individuals were not investing in the community.

Poole saw an opportunity to extend the SVP model to India. By that time, SVP already existed in a few other countries and was a model that could encourage these individuals to become engaged and invest money at the same time. After meeting with several of Venkatesan's high–net worth friends in Bangalore, he convinced Venkatesan to become the chair of SVP India, and in Bangalore the effort was launched.

Seventy SVP partners were recruited within the first twelve months, making Bangalore the fastest-growing chapter ever. Today, SVP India has expanded to five cities and adopted a dual approach in their investment strategy. Each city has its own unique local focus: Bangalore, for example, is focused on city cleanliness and garbage collection. Collectively, however, SVP India also has a national goal to catalyze livelihoods at the bottom of the economic pyramid by creating one million jobs. In the five cities, there are 250 SVP partners investing their capital, time, and acumen to make a difference.

Make Money and Make a Difference

After the 2008 financial crisis, nonprofits around the world were feeling the pain. When people's personal fortunes had decreased by 40 percent, there was little room for substantial philanthropy. At the same time, questions were raised about the effectiveness, efficacy, and impact of organizations promoting social and environmental causes. Philanthropists and other investors were exploring other models, whether it was earned income as part of a nonprofit's strategy, or impact investing, where an investment in a social enterprise could lead to both social impact and financial returns.[7] Not all social problems can be addressed through these new models, however, so conventional philanthropy will continue to play a major role.

"There are some problems that can only be solved by writing checks; I know of no impact investing model that will address the homelessness problem here in Seattle," Poole told me as he pointed outside his office window during our interview. Seattle's Pioneer Square is full of homeless people, as there are several community service centers located in this vicinity. Poole has a strong conviction that "what can be done with a for-profit business model must be done that way, and only after you have exhausted that possibility should you consider doing something on a purely nonprofit basis." The term *impact investing* was coined in 2007, but the practice was developed years earlier, with the rise of investors seeking both financial returns and social impact in such target areas as health, education, clean energy, and sustainable agricultural practices. To support this growth, several national and global organizations were established, including the Global Impact Investing Network. Their studies show that, since 2008, more than $500 billion has been invested in companies doing social and environmental good, and that number is expected to reach a trillion by 2020. Today, many established financial institutions have impact investment funds.[8]

As a senior Microsoft executive working with and learning from Bill Gates, Poole was profoundly inspired when Gates took his enormous talents from technology leadership to work full-time at the Bill and Melinda Gates Foundation, tackling and making significant progress on major problems of our time. As Poole moved into a phase of his life to extend the common good, Poole asked Gates to invest in the Unitus Seed Fund. Poole and his partner, Dave Richards, launched the fund in 2012 to prove that impact investing could work in India: investing in smart people in India to solve major societal problems and make money.

Unitus Seed Fund, now Unitus Ventures,[9] attracted capital from the Susan and Michael Dell Foundation, the famed Silicon Valley investor Vinod Khosla, and current and former Microsoft executives. The goal was to invest in early-stage Indian technology start-ups, primarily in health care, education, and financial sectors that serve middle- and low-income consumers. The success of Unitus Ventures has led Poole and Richards to launch a global effort to unlock billions of dollars of capital to flow into emerging markets, where most of the world's population is located and the need is greatest.

Unicorns at the Bottom of the Pyramid

As Unitus Ventures grew, Poole and Richards were being asked to expand their fund to serve other emerging markets. They were getting signals that other parts of the world also had amazing entrepreneurial talents and that these entrepreneurs could also benefit from access to capital and extend the common good. Jack Knellinger joined as their third managing partner, and he spent nine months traveling the world, exploring the possibility of creating an impact investment fund in other areas. What he found is that there were investors in other parts of the world supporting early-stage companies, but many lacked capital, especially operational capital, to launch their impact investment funds. Poole, Richards, and Knellinger thought that with the infusion of capital and by providing training they could support these funds to get started and succeed.

Capria Ventures was born. Capria Ventures invests in other fund managers or financial intermediaries and, using their global knowledge and an understanding of best practices in the world of impact investing, helps them succeed. Capria Ventures was born out of the idea of scaling the concept of impact investing in emerging markets in a way that embraces the differences in markets and building the capacity of high-caliber individuals.

It is hard to convince people to risk capital outside of mainstream ideas and markets, according to Poole. Trillions of dollars of wealth have been created in Silicon Valley and little of it has any connection to emerging markets. Entrepreneurs can service the US and Western markets from the comfort of Silicon Valley. "You do not have to fly to Indonesia to find the next unicorn if you can invest in one by driving down the street for five minutes," he says. Those trying to mobilize both talent and capital must recognize the difficulty of that challenge. They need ways to help investors make this leap of faith to put their money to work in India, Indonesia, Brazil, or anywhere else. Without building metrics, awareness, and trust, investors will not be convinced. Poole has used his investor and impact acumen to create an investment platform that channels capital and builds the capacity of impact investors in emerging markets. Together, they are extending the common good by supporting new education opportunities for low income people, access to affordable but quality health care, and access to alternative clean energy sources, in Africa, Asia, and Latin America. Poole is effectively using his growth mindset to convince enlightened investors he can make them money and have a positive impact on the world. He hopes to do this work for the next twenty-five years or more, well into his eighties and nineties: "I am not getting any younger every day, but it feels great to have a long-term mission ahead, one that I know can make incremental progress, one that I know other people want to join. That feeling of long-term purpose is important to me."

Applying Heart and Science

Thousands of kids graduate every summer, and many take some time off to figure out what they want to do next. Tony Mestres graduated as a history major with a minor in philosophy. After graduation, he traveled around the country and found his way back to New York City where he had grown up. There was no inkling in his background that he would become one of the philanthropic leaders of this country. One morning, Mestres's father handed him a copy of the Help Wanted section of the *New York Times*. The message was clear: it was time for Tony to find his next endeavor in life and begin his journey to adulthood. Today, he is the president and CEO of the Seattle Foundation, a community foundation with a $1 billion asset base. Mestres's journey began in the 1980s when he got a job at Bell South, a major telephone company, as a regional sales representative providing mobile data solutions to businesses. He excelled at his job and soon found himself in a sales management position in Midtown Manhattan.

That began a journey that lasted twenty-two years, fifteen of which were at Microsoft. Mestres learned as much as possible, trying to make an impact at an intersection of communications and computing. Mestres's first job at Microsoft was working with the Network Solutions Group. This is where he developed his business acumen and skills around negotiations, management, investments, and managing the performance of those investments.

At the same time, Mestres was also introduced to the Microsoft employee giving campaign. He says that the campaign showed "a broad esprit de corps and a set of principles for the company that were attractive to me." To Mestres, this was more than just a giving campaign; he began to understand that it was part of a broader set of cultural support mechanisms and management support mechanisms that provided him with an opportunity to "build myself as an individual in ways that I hadn't." All these activities put him in contact with other people in the company whom he respected, and he saw that they were also investing their time and money to better the community and doing great things. A small flame had been ignited!

In this quest to become a better individual and invest in the good of the community, he met with Paul Shoemaker around 2000 and joined Social Venture Partners. As an SVP partner, he was introduced to a nonprofit that needed marketing and business development support. The Kindering Center helps special needs infants and children and their families, and it is one of the leading neurodevelopment organizations in the world.

"As a thirty-something middle manager Microsoft guy who thought he was swashbucklingly capable, I suddenly was struck by an imposter's dilemma after meeting with the Kindering Center's executive director, Mimi Siegel," Mestres says. Siegel was a capable, experienced, and highly respected nonprofit leader. Mestres's insecurities concerned whether he could help this organization because he had no expertise in this field. He remembers Siegel giving him material and a videotape to get better insights into Kindering's work. The video brought him to tears, as he was about to become a new father and the mission related to children was so compelling. The video featured a mother who said, "Because of Kindering Center I saw for the first time my three-year-old son smile." This was a conversion experience for Mestres: he realized that investing his time and resources with Kindering would help him grow and have some positive impact, and it would also help him break out of a mold of a Microsoft guy focused solely on the corporate mission. Mestres is now the president emeritus of Kindering's board of directors.

This experience of working at Kindering and SVP gave him opportunities to grow his impact and influence within Microsoft over the next fifteen years, to learn from incredible mentors, and to observe how the founders of the company lived their lives. Mestres's career progressed in wonderful ways at Microsoft: he learned a great deal, had success, made mistakes, but continued to grow. He was proud to be working for a company he considers the greatest in the history of humankind. At the same time, Mestres was engaged more in the community. Eventually, he served as a board member of Social Venture Partners, which gave him additional skills he was able to bring to the Seattle Foundation.

After fifteen years at Microsoft, Mestres started a journey to explore life outside of the company. Many of his colleagues were convinced he would work for either Amazon or Google. As for Mestres, he genuinely had no idea of his future plans. As Mestres set a date to exit Microsoft, he was approached by an exciting startup, as well as a large defense contractor, offering jobs three times his Microsoft salary. Microsoft offered him a year's leave of absence to consider his next steps. Mestres almost took the offer but eventually decided he had to make the terrifying and financially illogical decision to leave the company.

His answer came quickly. The Seattle Foundation asked if he wanted to become their new CEO. After three and a half months, Mestres moved from the corporate world to the philanthropic sector. He also moved from a global role into a very specific, local one. "As somebody who had been an American history and philosophy major, I was fascinated by the role of government and the role of the private sector in society," he told me. The role offered Mestres an opportunity to work at an organization that was having a positive effect on the issues of wealth and inequality in society, and he would get to play a potentially meaningful role at its helm.

The move from a corporate sector into philanthropy has always been fraught with failures, as business leaders try to apply their growth mindset to issues that are complex and require subtlety in management, sometimes at the expense of efficiency. During Mestres's interview at the Seattle Foundation, Martha Choe, the foundation's chair and the former chief administrative officer of the Bill and Melinda Gates Foundation, asked him what he would leave behind in Redmond (Microsoft headquarters). That was a fascinating question. Mestres's reply showed how much he had learned with his role at Social Venture Partners and with the Kindering Center. He replied, "I have learned a lot in my role as a manager over fifteen years at Microsoft that could be applied to this new role, but it would have to be different in some way. I do not want to emulate a culture that was working on selling software and bring that into an organization that is trying to support the community and, in some ways, saving lives."

He explained to me how he continued to evolve his skills to be more effective rather than just efficient. As an illustration, he said if he walked into a room at Microsoft and saw twenty people trying to make a decision that only three people should be making, he would ask the other seventeen people to leave and go back to their work. Everyone would recognize that was a productive leadership decision. At the Seattle

Foundation, however, he was confronted with a similar situation where a room full of people were trying to decide which pictures to include in the annual report. One person who worked on the basic needs program was in the room helping with the decisions. Mestres's first inclination was to ask that person to leave, as the marketing folks were in the room and they needed to make the recommendations. It turned out the basic needs program officer was there because she had to ensure the images of the foundation's clients were not used in an exploitative manner. Mestres realized that if he had chased her back to her station, she would have left the organization.

Mestres has brought significant change to Seattle Foundation. He says he believes the old order of philanthropy, charities, and nonprofits as stop-gap efforts for human suffering no longer works. In an era where inequities have widened, systems change is necessary to close the inequity gap.

He has also brought to the foundation the Microsoft culture of openness, of debating assumptions, and of encouraging people to speak. Mestres helps the staff and the board rethink everything they are doing and why they are doing it. Their mission is to ignite powerful, rewarding philanthropy in the region and to create a vibrant and stronger community for all. He has introduced a new approach called "heart and science," which is now part of Seattle Foundation tagline. The genesis of the mantra "the heart and science of philanthropy" was a realization that ineffectiveness was born of one of two things: (1) leaning too much on the heart, which does not necessarily correlate to positive systems change that can affect people's lives at scale; or (2) leaning too much on the purely empirical left-brain attitude and strategies that do not appreciate deeply human needs, like learning from the community what they need as opposed to you telling them what they need.

This, to me, encapsulates the shift from a growth mindset to a purpose mindset—it is the bringing together of one's heart, empathy, values, principles, humility, and relationships with the best of social science thinking around strategies, policy, advocacy, grant making, and new models of investing. According to Mestres, Seattle Foundation is the place "that is succeeding in creating a place where there is an appropriate balance of

heart and science with a respect for both and a realization that one without the other is missing a major element."

Mestres is on a journey to provide strategies to deal with the existential
crises we face as a society and to figure out a way to address the wealth gap
in a way that appreciates we live in a capitalist democracy. According to
Mestres, "Wealth is growing at 8 or 9 percent in our country, and only 1.2
percent of that wealth is being deployed towards any type of social good.
And a great amount of the wealth that is being deployed towards social
good is going towards universities and hospitals." Mestres has nothing
against universities and hospitals and recognizes that they have the capacity to absorb large investments. Mestres and the Seattle Foundation are
working at two levels; one is improving the capacity of nonprofits to have
more measurable results; and the second is developing new investment
vehicles to encourage new donors and to drive increased generosity. He
is honoring the legacy and principles of a seventy-five-year-old institution
and evolving it to become an innovative civic and thought leader aimed
at addressing society's inequities.

If Mestres can succeed in doing that, he will have created a model that
can help heal societal divisions, a model that can be used by community
foundations around the country. He hopes that under his leadership, the
Seattle Foundation will continue to be the honest broker between those
who have the greatest financial capacity and those who are most in need
of opportunity, straddling political and geographical differences toward a
common way.

Five Loaves and Two Fishes

I met Margo Day on New Year's Eve at her beautiful home overlooking
Puget Sound. She graciously hosted me for the interview, even though she
was recovering from knee surgery after breaking her leg. In her light-filled
home on a rainy day, she told me how she had lived a purpose-driven life
driven by her faith and belief in the story of Jesus feeding five thousand
people with just five loaves and two fishes. "The story is about seeing a
huge need, having only a few resources but, driven by love offering those
resources to God to use. And when you do, miracles happen."

Day grew up as a shy middle-class kid in Colorado and Bellevue, Washington. She was fortunate enough to have her teachers, pastors, and others take an interest in her. Day recalls how her third-grade teacher asked her to do a volcano experiment in front of the entire school: "This shy little kid loves math and science, and I'm just going to give her an opportunity to blossom." Day says, "She was really the first adult influencer in my life that saw something in me." Her dad also had a strong influence over her life, instilling the idea that "your word is your bond," something she still lives by. Though her parents were not outwardly affectionate, they loved their children unconditionally. God was in the center of this family.

When Day turned eighteen in 1977, she was attending a church that had an outreach focus and had a forward-looking pastor who was convinced that electronic medical records and patient data would soon become important; he wanted to create electronic records of their missionary work in medical clinics in Venezuela. Knowing Day's interest in math and science, he asked if she would help develop a computerized data system. That's how she had her first taste of programming and learned how to code.

This work took her to San Diego, where she enrolled in Mesa Community College and started looking for work to help pay for her schooling. Though she had learned how to code, she soon found her calling to be business after answering an advertisement seeking a manager of a local franchise for Software City. An orthodontist in Southfield, Michigan, had acquired this franchise as a retirement plan and hired the twenty-five-year-old Day to run the business.

Seizing Opportunities

Over three years, Day built a $4 million business with operating margins of 35 percent by keeping a focus on the needs of the customer and developing superior service. It was unusual, to say the least, that someone two thousand miles away had handed a twenty-five-year-old the reins of his business and retirement nest egg. Day cut her teeth in this hypercompetitive environment, working by day and going to community college at night. She was about to be made a co-owner in the business when fate intervened.

Day's mother suffered a stroke, so she decided to return home. Back in Bellevue, she used her connections in the software industry to land a job at Micro Rim, which had offices on what eventually became the Microsoft campus. Day eventually landed a job at Lotus Development Corporation in 1988 and worked on Lotus Notes in 1991. Day followed a key principle of building relationships: "I always wanted to ensure that whomever I was talking to I was bringing something of value to them. I was not just building a personal connection but also creating a value connection. . . . You have to see what the other person is trying to accomplish and get in their shoes and see the world from their lens and then figure out what value you can add."

Though Lotus Notes was acquired by IBM in 1995, Day continuously built bigger partnerships for the company, and her role also expanded. By 1998, she felt she was "growing long in the tooth" and began searching for new and more challenging opportunities. A friend put her in touch with a recruiter at Microsoft, which was looking for senior women with expertise in business-channel development for small- and medium-sized businesses.

I Don't Want to Work for Microsoft

Microsoft was already a behemoth, so Day was not interested. "My perception of Microsoft at that time was individuals get rewarded, and I was not sure I would fit here," says Day. Her friend insisted, however, and Day eventually agreed to an interview. She met Kevin Johnson, who was then the corporate VP for global sales and now is the CEO of Starbucks. During their conversation, she realized that her vision of what Microsoft should do to compete with IBM and Oracle by building partner networks was similar to the strategy that Johnson was outlining. After meeting with the senior HR leadership and becoming convinced that Microsoft was indeed on a path from an individual win-lose culture to a team culture, Day decided to join, in 2001, to rebuild Microsoft's US business partner network. She says, "I was going to come in and not only help the business but help the culture and help the people."

She says that "every person I talked to at Microsoft came because they wanted to make a difference." So she set out to build a culture where people felt they were heard and respected and were a part of creating the vision. "If you can set the right tone," she says, "people will rally behind you and move mountains." Joining Microsoft at a senior level was difficult, especially the first three months. "It was like running up the steepest sand dune in the tightest fitting dress in high heels," she says with a laugh. Microsoft, however, also gave her the latitude and support so she could make the right business decision and also deliver the bad news when necessary.

The employee giving campaign offered Day the opportunity to build another level of purpose for employees on her team. She had a team across the United States, so she had become particularly skilled at encouraging her team to support their own preferred causes. "The ten-thousand-dollar match was a tremendous gift," she says, because it allowed money to go where the employees wanted it to go. For all the pressure and grind of running a growth business, becoming involved in the employee giving campaign was a release that allowed employees to make a difference outside of the company. "It made people feel that they were able to see more of their whole selves in the business as opposed to just your business role," she says.

Calling to Do Something Big

When Day turned fifty in 2009, she felt called to do something beyond what she was already contributing. "There was this stirring deep in my soul," she says, "and I had to do something big." She just did not know what it was, but the story of Five Loaves and Two Fishes was echoing in her heart. She became reacquainted with World Vision[10] when her younger brother went to work for the organization. She decided to go on vacation to Africa and offered World Vision four days of her time to visit one of their projects. World Vision chose Kenya and took her to see a water project they were working on in a community in West Pokot county 250 miles north of Nairobi in the semiarid Rift Valley.

On the first day in this remote area, World Vision hosted a devotional prayer, as the organization does at the start of every visit. A young Kenyan man started out by saying, "God put in my heart to tell the story of the five loaves and two fishes to feed 5,000 people." Day was stunned: halfway around the world, God was speaking to her through this boy, and she knew God wanted her to do something big here.

They visited the water project, an amazing piece of engineering to bring fresh water to sixty thousand people in this remote area suffering from a drought. Day also visited a project involving survivors of HIV/AIDS and one providing economic empowerment opportunities for people with disabilities. On the final day of her trip, World Vision took Day and her niece to visit a rescue center for girls. On the way, Day wanted to know what the girls were being rescued from, and she was told that these were girls who had escaped early forced marriage and female genital mutilation. This is a prevalent practice in many traditional communities, especially in Africa and in this tribe. Girls as young as eight to ten years old were forced to undergo female circumcision before their arranged marriage.

In a cinder block building, Day met thirty-four girls and listened to their stories of escape. "Harrowing is too small a word," she says. That is when she realized she could have been one of those girls, if not for the birth lottery of being born where she was born and with parents who cared for her, educated her, and gave her so many opportunities. She saw a fierce determination in these girls' eyes as they recounted their stories. This fierce determination was to have a better life even though they were aware of the repercussions they would face if caught.

Day discovered there were no secondary schools for the girls in this area as they all were married by that age and had children as early as twelve years old. That is when Day decided that she would build a school for the girls. She worked with World Vision, and they developed a plan. They estimated that it would cost $400,000 to build a secondary school for two hundred girls. World Vision asked her to fund half the costs and help raise the other half.

When Day returned from Kenya and went back to work, all she could talk about to her Microsoft colleagues were the girls she had met and her plans for the school. The employee giving campaign was beginning in October, so several of Day's colleagues joined to support her effort. "I had been very private about my philanthropy and did not want to impose," she says. But a few wanted to lean in. "I came to realize that I might be giving them a gift, so philanthropy started to take on this very interesting dimension." They raised the money in a short period using the Microsoft match and Day's own generous contribution. The first classroom at St. Elizabeth Girls Secondary School opened in 2010, and all the buildings were finished and formally commissioned in May 2011.

The Global Give Back Circle

I introduced Linda Lockhart to Day in 2011, as I felt there were synergies between the work they were doing. Lockhart is a force of nature who has been working in Kenya with girls. She provides them with economic opportunities during the gap year these girls are required to take after high school and before college. Many of these girls are married and never have a chance to go to college. The Global Give Back Circle[11] provides training and connects the girls to other women mentors to help them learn skills before they enter college. I met Lockhart in 2008 and was intrigued by her work and the opportunity to have women employees at Microsoft volunteer their time to mentor these girls, either through Skype or by just exchanging letters. Microsoft started partnering with the Global Give Back Circle after that meeting.

Lockhart and Day immediately hit it off. Day saw the Global Give Back Circle as a model to be adopted for the girls at the St. Elizabeth Girls Secondary School she had helped create. Lockhart loved the idea; on her next visit to Kenya, she visited the St. Elizabeth Girls Secondary School in the West Pokot area in the Rift Valley. Global Give Back Circle programs are optimized for a more urban environment, where there is connectivity and opportunities for mentors to communicate with the girls. But Lockhart fell in love with World Vision's Kenya Child Protection and

Education Project, and the two were determined to find a way to expand the Global Give Back Circle to the St. Elizabeth Girls Secondary School.

In partnership with World Vision, and with support from Day and the Microsoft women mentors, the mentorship program has taken root in West Pokot. "It's a divine intervention," Day says. "These connections have opened so many doors—it has been a watershed moment." Girls from Nairobi started visiting the St. Elizabeth Girls Secondary School and became mentors. Girls in their own country are now supporting other girls, thereby expanding the circle even more.

In less than a decade since Day's first visit to West Pokot, the impact of her work has been jaw dropping. The incidences of genital mutilation dropped from approximately 100 percent to under 15 percent. Day quickly reminds me, however, that the project is not just about eliminating female genital mutilation. The success is a by-product of their comprehensive approach. This approach has included community education and awareness, economic empowerment for the former circumcisers, and the Global Give Back Circle program. This program is beginning to provide an economic engine for impoverished families so they can see that educating their girls is better than the old way of marrying them off at a young age for a dowry.

The community is now benefiting from some of the girls who ran away and returned to help rebuild their communities. Faith was one of the girls Day met in 2009. Faith was married in 2019 to a man she met in church, whom she chose and loves, says Day with pride. Faith became a member of the Global Give Back Circle, went to college, obtained vocational skills, made money, reconciled with her parents, and built them a house.

Lillian was another one of the girls who sang for Day and shared her story when she visited in 2009. Lillian was a leader: she motivated other girls to escape with her. Day mentored Lillian through the Global Give Back Circle, and had the honor to attend her marriage and presented the couple with a cow. Like Faith, Lillian has broken the cycle of forced arranged marriages, and married a man whom she chose and loves. Lillian is quite the entrepreneur; she has a degree in hospital records management and IT. She also has a haircutting business and supports her mother with the profits from rooms she has built on a small parcel of land and rents out to students. "The community is seeing this," Day says, "and they realize that the future in this way is far better than the past of what they experienced."

Can You Dream Big?

With the success of World Vision's Kenya Child Protection and Education Project, World Vision has developed a larger effort to eliminate female genital mutilation in Kenya. There are many counties in Kenya where the prevalence of this practice is more than 80 percent. Day was asked to join this effort. Day stood at a crossroads: she had the most amazing job, but she also had an opportunity to dream big and have an immense impact. Day eventually decided she could not work full-time and support a big project with World Vision, so she retired early from Microsoft, in 2018. She had a fabulous team in place and knew she could step away, and there was a deep bench to take over. Today, she is focused on working with World Vision on the first phase of the Big Dream Project, a $30 million effort. She has made a large financial commitment of her Microsoft stocks that she held on to over her seventeen-year career.

"I was a shy, introverted kid who had no choice as to the family she was born into. I had opportunities and doors opened for me, and so this wealth isn't mine," she says. As our time came to a close, she choked up. "I do not know what greater gift one could have than to impact someone else's life." Day was living the life of her dreams before her fiftieth birthday, but her life now is a thousand times better. Just before I visited her, it was midnight in Kenya, so she was receiving all these messages wishing her a Happy New Year and giving her blessings. "Just to be part of the world community," she says. "That's a life worth living."

CHAPTER FIVE

Climbing the Second Mountain

David Brooks chronicles his journey toward faith in *The Second Mountain*. It is a personal reflection of his journey from being self-centered with an unrelenting focus on power, achievement, and self-gratification to the "second mountain" of gratitude, delight, and kindness that springs from a life devoted to service. He also highlights how so many of us pursued a career, raised a family, became successful, and then decided to move beyond personal growth and success, to embrace a deeper journey. We have an epiphany, seize a new opportunity, try something new, or experience the unexpected, causing us to pause and seek alternatives. The difference between the first mountain and the second is a shift from acquisition to contribution. "Our individualistic culture inflames the ego and numbs the spirit," Brooks writes.[1] Young people throughout history have been changemakers. Mahatma Gandhi, the Rev. Martin Luther King Jr., Kailash Satyarthi and Malala Yusufzai (2014 Nobel Peace Prize winners), and currently Greta Thunberg have all been at the forefront for leading massive movements of change at a very young age. These individuals developed a strong sense of purpose early on and with great courage acted on it. In each, however, there was an incident that drove them to act and ignited their purpose. For example, Satyarthi, trained as an engineer, left that career to publish a magazine that documented incidents of kids in child slavery and exploitation in India. An appeal by a father to help find his abducted daughter led him in his midtwenties to found Bachpan Bachao Andolan (Save Childhood Movement) to rescue children and their families from the shackles of slavery and pave the way for their reintegration into mainstream society. He led the largest global march against child labor, which spanned 103 countries—one of the largest social movements ever on behalf of exploited children.[2]

Greta Thunberg, the Swedish teenage environmental activist, has gained international recognition for her work on promoting the perils of climate change. At age fifteen, she skipped school on Fridays to protest outside the Swedish Parliament calling for stronger action on climate change. She is now the face of young climate change activists all around the world and has launched the "school strike for climate" movement around the world.

These individuals did not choose between climbing the first or second mountain; they discovered the bonds between self and society, and their life's mission, very early on. For others, that spark happens later in life.

Having grown up in India, I am not fully steeped in Judeo-Christian philosophy. As I reflected on my journey, I wondered if I was now on the second mountain. Brooks cautions us not to take the metaphor too literally. He says there is no one formula for your second mountain. I have taken several different paths that have led to personal growth and happiness and the joy derived from contributing to society. I am no saint and have doubts about my success—nor am I motivated by some higher moral calling. I have tried, however, to consciously continue what I enjoy doing, taking on the challenge of experiencing and learning through new opportunities, while at the same time leaving room to contribute to the common good. There is no guarantee that everything I have done has led to the common good; mistakes have been made and hopefully I have learned from them and moved forward with a better or refined approach.

Arpita and Rajeev Agarwal are climbing in some ways both mountains; whereas Akila and Soma Somasegar have developed a great partnership in which they are taking each other's success on different mountains and together are both acquiring and contributing. The individuals I cover in this chapter all have had their personal success through what David Brooks terms *acquisition* and are now in the contributing phase of their journey. I am not sure any of them see it that way. None of them have fallen off a peak to climb the second peak, but all of them have, because of their time at Microsoft, become interested in a collective purpose. Some have created a new common purpose, and others have joined forces to continue to drive for the betterment of society.

Conquering the Chaos

In *Revolution from Above: India's Future and the Citizen Elite*, acclaimed sociologist and author Dipankar Gupta argues that at every moment when democracy has made significant advances, it was the citizen elite who led the charge, often going against the grain of popular demands and sentiments. He offers compelling evidence that democracy does not reflect reality as much as it shapes and changes it. These citizen elites have intervened actively with a vision for strengthening democracy rather than for short-term electoral gains. During my interview with Ravi Venkatesan, the former chairman of Microsoft India and the author of *Conquering the Chaos: Win in India, Win Everywhere*, he shared how Dipankar's book had a profound impact on his outlook and how he should spend the rest of his life.

He agreed with Dipankar's thesis that India has not delivered meaningfully in terms of universal health, education, and livelihood and that it, too, needs a citizen elite to initiate change. Venkatesan also agreed that this change requires visionary leaders and cannot be contemplated through the short-term rationality of elections. After leaving Microsoft, Venkatesan's first project was to write *Conquering the Chaos*, meant to help global companies like Microsoft and others navigate an extremely challenging market. It also coincided with giant corruption scandals in India. During Venkatesan's US book launch in New York, US ambassador to India Frank

Wisner asked him, "What happens if the chaos actually engulfs India and then global companies pack their bags and leave?" That question drove Venkatesan to ask why India fails to live up to its potential.

He decided to put the common good above self-interest by mobilizing people he knew with power, wealth, and influence to launch Social Venture Partners (SVP) in Bangalore, India. As I mentioned earlier, SVP is a collection of individuals, volunteers, parents, community leaders, and philanthropists who commit their time, talent, and treasure to collectively work to create a better and more just tomorrow.[3]

I met Venkatesan when I joined Microsoft in June 2004. He had joined a few months before me as the chairman of Microsoft India. I had the privilege of working with him as we launched several new initiatives in India, including Project Shiksha, which enables government teachers to integrate technology into their teaching. Since its launch in 2003, more than nine thousand teachers have been trained, and 430,000 students have benefited from the improved, fun-filled, and interactive learning environment these teachers create.[4] I also worked with Venkatesan to help launch the Microsoft employee giving campaign in India. Venkatesan wanted to launch this program because, although Microsoft was at the height of its powers, it had a less-than-stellar reputation in India. He worked on various initiatives to earn trust on behalf of the company. Furthermore, he found that, though many employees were young and bright, a sense of entitlement had crept into company culture, captured by the attitude of "what has the company done for *me* lately?"

The employee giving campaign addressed both of these issues. Employees would be engaged in the community, becoming brand ambassadors by contributing to their community and to other causes important to them. Microsoft India's leadership became role models through their deep involvement and caring approach. Soon after its launch, almost 55 percent of employees participated in the program.

After leaving Microsoft, Venkatesan turned away from other CEO positions and became part of the Unitus Ventures, launched by Microsoft colleague Will Poole (chapter 4), and supported the effort in India to support early-stage impact ventures. This involvement helped Venkatesan gain deeper insights into the social-impact development space from an investment perspective. Both his experience with Unitus and SVP India—now in seven cities with more than two hundred SVP partners to impact the lives of thousands of people across India—is what led him to his two new efforts. As SVP matured, Venkatesan became curious about and challenged by large-scale societal issues. "There is so much more I had to solve than just building a business that I had done multiple times. So I just found it to be more challenging and stimulating to work on more urgent issues, and it's much more rewarding." Even though he is not as wealthy as his other Microsoft colleagues, he told me he has enough and does not need to work for money. He decided to focus his attention, talent, and networks on solving major world problems.

Catalyzing an Entrepreneurial Movement of Youth

Venkatesan is now focused on two primary efforts. First, he launched the Global Alliance for Mass Entrepreneurship (GAME) with a goal of enabling ten million young people from ages eighteen to twenty-nine to start businesses instead of looking for jobs. He hopes half will be women and that these youth, in turn, will create fifty million jobs by 2030. The second effort is becoming the special representative at UNICEF, where he is shaping a new global initiative called Generation Unlimited.[5] The goal is to prepare youth ages ten to twenty-four to transition successfully to different types of work and become engaged citizens.

In India, there are simply not enough formal-sector jobs (jobs that are taxed, monitored by government, and included in the country's gross national product [GNP] or gross domestic product [GDP]) for the size of the youth population. Almost one million young people turn eighteen in India every month and are obviously looking for jobs. Another seven to eight million people move from rural India to cities, also looking for work. India must, therefore, create eighteen to twenty million jobs every year. According to Venkatesan, the formal sector is 10 percent of the economy and has created almost zero net new jobs despite growth from productivity gains, a challenge that will increase along with greater automation. He also says millions more small businesses must be started with the hope that they will become medium-sized companies, thereby producing many new jobs. Though the growing start-up economy delivers financial value, it does not deliver enough jobs: by 2020, there will be 10,500 start-ups, but they will deliver just two hundred thousand jobs, which is only a drop in the bucket for India.[6] In most countries, small- and medium-sized companies (SMEs) drive employment; in India, only 21 percent of nonfarm employees work in SMEs. In China and the United States, for example, 82 percent and 53 percent of nonfarm labor, respectively, work in SMEs. Edmund Phelps, the 2006 Nobel laureate in Economics and the author of *Mass Flourishing*, says, "Most innovation (and job creation) wasn't driven by a few isolated visionaries like Henry Ford and Steve Jobs; rather, it was driven by millions of people empowered to think of, develop, and market innumerable new products and processes, and improvements to existing ones [in their local communities]."

GAME is trying to change this dynamic by focusing on supporting youth to create "mass entrepreneurs," people who hire five to twenty other people and serve a local community need. For example: building contractors, registered mom-and-pop stores, small professional service firms, small exporters, and framer and artisan collectives. With a large number of educated youth—almost eight million graduate secondary schools and three million graduate college every year—there is a need to provide skills training, shifting their mindset toward work, and providing role models through mentorship programs. India ranks a respectable thirty-eighth out of 124 countries on an individual risk acceptance for entrepreneurship on the global entrepreneurship index.[7]

One exciting experiment Global Alliance and the New Delhi school system have started is to make entrepreneurship a required eighth- to twelfth-grade subject; this affects 750,000 youth. They have also created incubators across rural India, where they are creating cohorts of young people by providing them mentorship and access to finance. Finally, they have partnered with several e-commerce platforms to get these new young entrepreneurs started, with a major focus on women. Only 8 percent of businesses in India are owned by women; in neighboring Bangladesh, that number is 35 percent.[8] GAME took the approach of focusing on "home entrepreneurship," which enables women to start and run businesses from home. This provides women an opportunity to get involved in the growing Indian economy without having to sacrifice raising kids or upsetting other cultural norms that might frown upon women working outside of the house.

The agenda is ambitious, but so is the opportunity. "If we can unlock the model successfully, we can then begin to scale them up to the kind of numbers that we hope to achieve," says Venkatesan confidently. Venkatesan returns to his theme of creating the right incentives to develop entrepreneurs but also to develop youth willing to invest in their communities.

Giving Agency—Inculcating Citizenship

Generation Unlimited is Venkatesan's second major effort.[9] UNICEF partners with the UN system and governments to mobilize and train job creators and prepare them to become engaged citizens. By 2030, two billion young people will be seeking opportunities for a bright future. The goal is to train youth in twenty solutions and initiatives that map onto the UN's Sustainable Development Goals[10] and also integrate into country-level investment priorities. Some of these programs include Alternative Learning Programs, Out of School Youth, SmartUp Factory, and Techno Girl, among others.

Generation Unlimited's Youth Challenge is another noteworthy effort, where youth join innovation workshops to design solutions to the challenges of their lives; the best idea in each country gets a small grant, expert advice, and mentoring. Then five winners are chosen and granted $20,000 to take their ideas to the next level with advanced mentorship. Generation Unlimited works with several government agencies, tapping into existing programs and mobilizing existing resources to gain momentum.

Venkatesan spoke at length about how he expects to reach the number of youth he wants to be trained and supported. Partnerships with governments at the local and national level are key. He was relatively unconcerned about the challenges of bureaucracy, graft, or corruption. Instead, the challenge is to leverage government programs, institutional machinery, and infrastructure to reach scale. Venkatesan also observed another challenge: some young people fear failure. Getting a job is a much safer option than starting a business; in many cases, a family's investment in education is their collective ticket out of poverty. Starting a business is a risky proposition. To mitigate this problem, GAME works with government agencies to create a social security program as a safety net for youth and help them overcome their fear of failure. In 2013, economists Ross Levine and Rona Rubenstein found that entrepreneurs do not have a special gene for risk—they come from families with money.[11] Financial stability is essential, and that is what government programs can help provide.

Furthermore, many governments have various financial support programs for small entrepreneurs. The key is to provide effective access to these programs. In April 2009, I visited a project that Microsoft had supported and was being implemented by the Aga Khan Rural Support Program in the state of Gujarat in western India. In Dedipada, a small village outside the town of Netrang, the technology center blackboard displayed a list of government job openings, along with commodity prices. One of the roles for the center community manager was to search the internet to find appropriate government programs for this community of farmers and buffalo herders. This linkage to government services was critical to the community's well-being. In the next village, the community was waiting to tell me the story of seventy-two buffalo.

The farmers had wanted to buy buffaloes and were trying to negotiate a price with the middlemen. But the community manager had another idea. He discovered a government program on the internet—the Swarna Jayanti Gram Swarozgar Yojana (SJGSY) scheme—that would allow the villagers to negotiate better prices as a group. This led to a significantly lower price, and they bought seventy-two buffalo. What's more, they were able to negotiate a much higher price for their milk from the milk cooperative—eighteen rupees instead of twelve rupees per liter. The middlemen who had previously taken their milk and delivered it to the cooperative had mixed it with water, thereby reducing the fat content and getting a much lower price. The farmers subsequently ordered a machine online that measured milk's fat content and then used the computer center to send the reading over the internet to the milk cooperative. The 50 percent increase in earnings had a significant economic impact on this tiny community.

Venkatesan has a clear dream scenario: "When a young person from the humblest of backgrounds feels empowered to pursue an idea, build a business, and create a solution, then we are supporting youth to be an army of changemakers. We want to move from the idea geography is your destiny to empowering millions of youth to unlock their own destiny, thereby catalyzing a social change movement."

Venkatesan is also concerned about the planet and humanity's tipping point. "When you look at climate change, the environment, issues around mass migration, the plastic crisis, the water crisis, and a growing list of them, the future truly rests on getting many, many, many, many more people to become problem solvers," he says. At this stage in his life, Venkatesan wants to be at the forefront of driving change. Someone with his level of power and influence has stepped up to apply his acumen and skills to ensure youth around the world will continue to have the opportunity to also apply their acumen and skills. Eventually, by all of us playing our small part, we can make positive change happen.

Getting Lost—Finding Purpose

I interviewed Bill Hilf in his top-floor office with a view of the Seattle Seahawks stadium and the Seattle waterfront. Hilf wore a Seahawks jacket, the city's beloved football team; he is the CEO of Vulcan, Paul Allen's management company that oversees a broad range of assets, businesses, and philanthropic work. Hilf's physique runs more toward a basketball player than a linebacker. As we sat down to chat, he shared that his life was shaped by two tragic events: losing his father at age seven and his older brother at age eight. Therefore, his siblings and mother became his rock, early in life. The loss of his father framed his view of who he could learn from and was a lifelong lesson that life can change dramatically and quickly.

Hilf has certainly climbed the first mountain with his successful software-building career at IBM, HP, and Microsoft. He rose through the ranks at Microsoft, becoming the general manager of the Windows and

Server Group, a big promotion from starting at the company as a technical program manager a few years before. He was now in charge of launching the new Windows Server 2008 product, a multibillion-dollar product line. His priority was to complete the project and launch on time. Though he was involved with philanthropy, he said his check-writing was "what I call pay-to-the-order-of"—more out of obligation than purpose or connection. "It was never really deeply wired into me."

Hilf's orientation transformed on a morning jog in Manila. Manila was his last stop on a one-month trip around the world for a series of customer and launch events. His admittedly terrible sense of direction led his morning jog into a barangay (a Tagalog name for an inner city neighborhood). He saw street kids playing basketball and joined just to have fun. Most of these kids were homeless and lived on the streets and played with any type of ball, often with a hoop nailed to a tree or the side of a building. During his business meetings that day, he kept thinking of these kids, so that evening he returned with a bunch of basketballs to give to the kids.

On his flight back home, he had an epiphany. He had to try to directly help these street children, despite the complexities of their lives, their environment, and level of poverty. When he spoke to his wife, she told him to find children—or a cause—closer to home. But he was convinced he needed to do something—maybe it was a white savior complex; so he called friends at Nike, and they shipped him dozens of fully inflated basketballs to his office at Microsoft in Redmond. He showed up in Manila with new shoes and basketballs for these kids. Of course, the kids sold the shoes and the basketballs. Money was crucial, and they had no need for new shoes. Hilf tried this for a year and finally realized just shipping basketballs and shoes into these communities was not going to solve the larger problems, and that fly-in philanthropy was not sustainable. He needed to partner with local organizations that were working with these kids full-time and within their neighborhoods, not as an outsider showing up from time to time.

Eventually, he started working with Teresa Silva, a local leader who had been providing health care, shelter, and education to street kids. Hilf agreed to support her work and start a sports program. He has been supporting the program for thirteen years now. High Five Hope is bringing the power of structured, supportive sports program to street children in the Philippines. It now includes volleyball for girls and *futkal*—a type of street soccer. High Five Hope has also expanded to Cebu in the central Philippines. They operate in two locations, including a program in a boy's prison. Sports are used as a teaching vehicle and provide scholarships for further education. Hilf says the reason he stuck with the program was that sports were the catalytic element that allowed him to survive and have hope when he was young: sports was a lifeboat.

Red to Yellow

Hilf remembers how Microsoft senior executives would take the Insight Assessment, a thinking-skills and mindset assessment,[12] coded by color. His test would always show red, which meant he led from the front, accomplished tasks, and was results oriented. Bill Gates and Steve Ballmer also got red, so he was very proud to be in their company. After his trip from Manila, his next assessment resulted in a leading yellow: a leadership style valuing empathy and collaboration. He was shocked, so he repeated the test. Again, it came out leading yellow. Subsequent tests continued to be yellow. The experience in Manila had transformed what was important to him.

In meetings at Microsoft in Redmond, where the most important conversations were about revenue per customer and technical capabilities, his mind kept shifting to what he experienced in the Philippines, where the problems for the street children are gruesome and severe, with young kids exposed and trapped in situations that are criminal and dark. He wanted to do more with his own and Microsoft's intellectual horsepower and capabilities.

During this time, Hilf became the executive sponsor for the UNHCR, where he was further exposed to how large organizations were trying to do good on an extreme scale. In this capacity, he visited refugee camps in Asia and Africa. During a visit to the Kakuma, a large refugee camp at the border of Sudan and Kenya, he saw how technology could provide significant improvement to people's lives there. He helped set up computer labs in these camps. A much thornier problem was developing a digital identification system for the millions of refugees who lack official identification. Even after multiple visits to Geneva to work with the tech teams at UNHCR, he could not develop a solution. The nonprofit and development community were at least ten years behind the tech community. Today, there are several organizations working to develop digital identities for refugees, including Microsoft and Accenture.[13]

He had difficulty wrapping his mind around the fact that the best and brightest engineers were creating things like new Instagram filters, but there was no motivation to work on the most important problems in the world. Fast-forward to 2013 when Hilf transitioned to Hewlett-Packard. There he continued to ruminate about this problem, deciding that whatever he would do next had to be more meaningful.

Joining the Renaissance

In 2016, Paul Allen interviewed Hilf to become the CEO of Vulcan. Hilf had not met Allen at Microsoft, given their different timelines. But through shared connections, he was introduced to Allen when Allen was searching for a CEO to run his companies. Hilf had an immediate connection with him over, for example, their shared angst and frustration about their seeming inability to use tech and data to create breakthroughs in areas such as conservation or climate change. Hilf was attracted to Allen's vision of building the capability to solve enormous problems. Given Allen's legendary technical skills and curious mind and his own experiences and frustrations, Hilf could not say no to the CEO position.

As CEO, Hilf oversees Allen's business interests and his philanthropic endeavors. In this role, he is tasked with guiding the company's diverse commercial and philanthropic endeavors—from capital investment and real estate to tackling climate change and improving conservation efforts and to promoting access to arts and culture. Hilf is proud of his work at Vulcan over the last four years. He says, "What we've been known for in many cases is that we do think heavily about technology and data and its ability to impact some of our planet's biggest challenges. We employ world-class engineers who work on these things directly. And we do think about what a much more impactful technology revolution for philanthropy could be."

This is what he wants to do for the rest of his life: use technology to help humans and the planet survive the massive existential threat of climate change, to better protect our oceans, wildlife and their ecosystems, and to help communities thrive. He has taken on the challenge of changing incentives for engineers and scientists to shift their focus to this type of problem-solving. For example, he has developed clever ways to persuade an outstanding machine-learning engineer to work at Vulcan, even though Amazon, Microsoft, and Google offer stock options. Like Soma Somasegar, he also has faith in the millennials driven by a sense of mission and not just economic incentives. Hilf took great pleasure in telling me a story about a highly successful young engineer at Microsoft who wanted to work at Vulcan on their climate project. Even though Hilf told her she would make four to five times more at Microsoft, she still wanted to work at Vulcan because of the climate project.

Hilf has discovered his purpose mindset; he confronted a world problem in a catalytic moment, a problem that pushed him beyond his own self-centered concerns. His story followed David Brooks's argument: "We are taught young to succeed and win at any cost and compete to have the most things and have the most dollars and material things, and now we perpetuate that with social media." Recognizing the value of humility is one way to combine the growth mindset with purpose and put them to use for a different set of rewards.

Hilf now enjoys tackling hard problems, like improving climate modeling to change the way we understand climate or using new types of data and machine learning to identify and predict natural disasters and environmental crimes. Though these are some of the most challenging problems that could take large investments and decades to solve, it provides Hilf a pure adrenaline rush. He must take a careful, surgical approach and put the best minds to work. "The aspirational scope is what really gets me most excited, and that will continue for a long time, as with Paul Allen's passing, it is our job to execute on Paul's vision."

No Boundaries

I took my first airplane ride in 1965 when I was ten when I flew from
Poona (Pune) to Bombay (Mumbai), a short thirty-minute flight; it was a
major achievement for me and my younger brother. I stepped foot on an
international flight in 1979 when I went to complete my architectural
internship in the neighboring country of Sri Lanka. I was lucky to get selected to visit Switzerland for a semester abroad experience in 1980, and
that then exposed me to the wonders of Europe. Since coming to the
United States in 1981, I have traveled all over the world and racked up
millions of miles. I went from being a very local kid with no outside personal exposure to a global citizen moving seamlessly across borders.

Not everyone has this opportunity. Forty percent of Americans have
never left the country and 54 percent have visited ten states or fewer.[14]
Claire Bonilla, on the other hand, grew up as an air force brat, experiencing life living in different countries. She lived a sheltered life, she tells me,
but was aware of a global culture and a world with no boundaries. She
grew up during a time of global change, with the end of the Cold War and
the fall of the Berlin Wall. She wanted to be part of that experience, to
witness change, to learn and listen. She studied German while living with
an exchange family and traveled through Russia and the newly formed
countries of the Eastern bloc.

Bonilla planned her education to allow her to better understand the
inflection points that were the catalyst for dramatic change. This built
her love for understanding systems, a competency she has carried across
her career. After graduating from the London School of Economics in
international studies, she was ready to apply her skills and began working
on her PhD. But she realized that with a PhD she would pigeonhole herself. So she took a break, fell in love with the Pacific Northwest, and
ended up working for Ernst & Young centered on their change management group. She learned about collaboration when she joined Microsoft
in 1999, where she managed the Exchange Partner Advisory Council with
top Microsoft partners to showcase Microsoft's most innovative products
and ideas.

Bonilla's growth mindset emerged through VP Ian Rogoff's sage advice. He recommended she move into a different business unit every two years, to get the most exposure and experience across the company. She took this advice to heart and moved into new roles where she met amazing people and learned from innovative leaders. Having a growth mindset helped Bonilla move up very quickly within the company.

Cultivating the Community

Bonilla was exposed to the Microsoft employee giving campaign early on. She was introduced to a different lifestyle from her middle-class upbringing when she started her work as a consultant for a Fortune 500 company. She stayed at five-star hotels and ate fancy meals with clients, experiences and a life she could only dream of previously. The late 1990s saw the height of the dot-com boom: Microsoft's stock was climbing and people felt wealthy. At the height of the giving campaign in October, however, Bonilla saw people engaged in the community. It was not just about giving money but about volunteering time and serving on nonprofit boards, for example. A new door opened, and she jumped into a movement that carried her along with it. She had a new mindset and fit into a new culture, never the result of any pressure.

Microsoft's message that you can change the world resonated with Bonilla. Though simple, it was also empowering: technology could help every person meet their potential. She also witnessed how this message transferred outside the workplace. At work, while your project would take time to come to fruition, you could also pursue that same purpose in a different, local way. "I am going to change my community. I am going to change my neighborhood, my Boys and Girls club, or I am going to do something big. This was at the heart of what drove folks at Microsoft," Bonilla says. She described her experience as an honor and a privilege to make a difference, even if it was only in a small way.

The Humanitarian Switchboard Operator

Bonilla's last role at Microsoft was leading the Humanitarian Disaster Response team. The moment a natural disaster struck, Microsoft employees would flood her with calls from around the world, asking how they could help. I chuckled as Bonilla described herself as a "humanitarian switchboard operator." My wife called me Microsoft's FEMA (Federal Emergency Management Agency), as I had to, in my role as the head of the company's philanthropy group, coordinate the company's response when an earthquake, tsunami, hurricane, wildfire, or other humanitarian disaster struck. My team worked closely with Bonilla's during these events. My team would coordinate the philanthropic response and her team would provide the cross-company disaster support to customers, employees, and partners.

She remembers employees telling her, "I'll work late into the night, I'll work weekends, just tell me what to do." Bonilla was humbled by the experience: "Here were some of the smartest people from all over the world with the biggest hearts saying, 'I am your tool, use me.'" During her eight years in this role, every time a disaster struck, an employee would write a thank-you note to her: "I have been in the company for eighteen years or so and getting ready to leave, and I am now going to stay, because I found a meaningful way to connect with the greater good, and this company put in the time and investment to allow me to engage."

After the Haiti earthquake in 2010, her team, in collaboration with different technology partners and Microsoft employees around the world, restored the country's IT infrastructure in four months and pushed them forward seventy years with the new technology installations. This collaboration with nonprofit partners and a consortium of technology and other companies brought together smart, skilled people to apply their growth mindset for a compelling humanitarian purpose.

As her unit and responsibilities grew, Bonilla missed having a direct impact on communities. She sought a new opportunity to apply her experience to the nonprofit sector and the global health space.

Wiping a Disease off the Planet

As Bonilla approached the midlife crisis year of age forty, she decided to spend the second half of her life helping in an area she could have an impact on. Bonilla had joined the board of the Washington Global Health Alliance to better understand the broader spectrum of global health issues and find out if she wanted to pursue her involvement further. During her time on the board, she met numerous Microsoft alumni who had "jumped ship" and were working on global health challenges, such as cold-chain storage delivery for vaccines in Africa. These conversations gave her the courage to leave Microsoft and climb her next mountain.

After evaluating several possible options, she chose SightLife, an organization devoted to eradicating corneal blindness. Though many people focused on large-scale impact issues like maternal health, population control, and health education, Bonilla chose the corneal blindness niche because 12.7 million people are affected, and it is the third leading cause of preventable blindness. Ninety-eight percent of those affected live in low- and middle-income countries. Corneal blindness is growing at the rate of 1.5 million cases per year, but she thought she could play a formative role in partnering with others to wipe this disease off the planet during her lifetime.

Monty Montoya, the former CEO and president of SightLife, also served on the board of Washington Global Health Alliance. Bonilla learned about the nonprofit through her interactions with Monty, fell in love with the organization, and then became its chief global officer. The jump from Microsoft to a nonprofit is never easy and took some time. Bonilla and her husband created a ten-year financial plan so she could walk away from Microsoft and not dramatically alter her children's lifestyle. She hastened to add, "We live very differently now, and it's the most rewarding job I have."

Mission Mindset to Purpose Mindset

As Bonilla left Microsoft to join a nonprofit with 177 employees, her challenge, first as chief global officer and then as CEO, was to apply what she had learned at Microsoft—a very large and resource-rich company—to a small, resource-constrained organization, where people were motivated by mission rather than return on investment. She offered foundational tools and brought in a business focus to a mission-driven culture. Bonilla explains that, at SightLife, "Everyone is mission-driven, everybody cares. That is why people come to work. We all want to do something to help the blind." But she says there's a big difference between a purposeful mission-driven culture and an intentional one. In mission-driven organizations, the tendency is to intervene where there is the most need (purposeful). In certain cases, however, it might make more sense to intervene where one can make the most difference (intentional). She also brought in how Microsoft intentionally chose to enter and stay in a market or to develop a market. When a small nonprofit works in low- and middle-income countries, Bonilla says it must understand return on investment better than anyone else. "We need to walk away from any investment if the return is not appropriate. The understanding of market analytics and segmentation models, especially in emerging markets, was one of the biggest tools that I was able to bring."

When Bonilla began, it cost $650 to deliver one cornea to a community. After two and a half years of applying her rigorous intentional and purposeful mindset, she was able to reduce the cost to $150 dollars per cornea. Her staff also had strong skills in cornea recovery, so she asked staff to take time out of their work (while still being paid) to travel to an eye bank in India or elsewhere and spend 10 percent of their time training staff in these locations to develop the same skills, thereby improving the sector. She believes that by 2040 there will be no surgical wait time for people suffering from corneal blindness and that education and innovation will eventually prevent the need for such surgery. Her organization's systems approach moved SightLife from an eye bank to an organization offering comprehensive services focused on the entire health system, including education, policy, and advocacy to create access to organ donations and to ensure no one suffers from corneal blindness.

Surviving a War to Lead a Movement

The Iran-Iraq war began on September 22, 1980, and lasted for eight years. Hadi Partovi and his twin brother, Ali, grew up during this time in Tehran. Partovi tells me that from age seven to eleven they would hide in the basement every night, ears covered, as bombs fell around them. The son of a physicist father and a computer scientist mother, his life trajectory changed when his parents brought home the Commodore 64 computer. "It had no games or software on it," he says. "I taught myself to code from a book." He spent time learning to code because there was nothing else to do in that environment. "For anybody who has the least amount of hope, computer programming is an escape, and it lets you realize one's dreams in a virtual world even if in the physical world you live in is not going well."

I had worked on a Commodore 64 in the early 1980s when I was a student at the Massachusetts Institute of Technology. I was thrilled when Partovi proudly showed me the Commodore 64 his father had restored. His father had saved the large floppy disks and their original lines of code written by the Partovi brothers while in Iran. After immigrating to the United States, Partovi spent his summers working as a software engineer to help pay his way through high school and college, and that is when he started realizing that coding skills were in such high demand that people were willing to do whatever they could to find talent.

No community of coders existed at Partovi's high school in New York during the late 1980s, so he was thrilled to meet many like minds when he studied computer science at Harvard from 1990 to 1994. When he arrived at Microsoft as an eighteen-year-old intern, it was the early days of Windows 1.0 and 2.0 and DOS. Apple was not yet a powerhouse, and Windows was not yet popular. That internship at Microsoft changed his life. As with others in this book, Partovi was struck by how smart his coworkers were, including his manager, Ben Slivka (also a major philanthropist in the Seattle area). He was so excited by the company and its products that he invested the $3,000 he saved as an intern, in Microsoft stocks.

After starting as an engineer, he rose through the Microsoft ranks quickly, becoming head of product program management, where he ran the Internet Explorer team. They were years behind Netscape in the "browser wars." "We had a much smaller team," he says, "but we had a tight-knit brilliant group of people—some of the smartest minds to basically win that browser war." A lesson he has carried with him: "Surround yourself with the smartest people—they can do much greater things than you can imagine."

Seeding a Computer Science Talent

Partovi caught the entrepreneurship bug and launched several start-ups. One, iLike, was acquired by MySpace,[15] and another, Tellme Networks, was acquired by Microsoft, both of which made him quite wealthy.[16] Over the past twenty years, Partovi also became an investor in and adviser to, start-ups. Partovi developed the acumen to invest in companies like Facebook (when they were only nine people) or in Dropbox (when it was only two people), as well as Airbnb, Uber, and Zappos. He consistently saw the same story of incredible opportunity for financial wealth and the ability to have a world-changing impact, yet these companies had difficulty finding talent due to a dearth of young people being exposed and trained in computer science.

In 2012, Hadi and his brother, Ali, launched Code.org with a dream "that every student should have the same basic opportunity to be introduced to computer science, not because every kid needs to become a coder, but because having an opportunity to decide if you're passionate about it, decide if it clicks with you, is an important part of figuring out your career." He went on to say, "The basic understanding of how technology works is changing society, and the ethical impacts of technology are important for civic engagement for every citizen." When I asked Partovi if the Microsoft employee giving program inspired him on this path, his honest answer was not in any life-changing sort of way. But he concurred that the energy around the giving campaigns in October was very visible: "It was not something buried on the website but was front and center with the top executives actively participating in it."

What did have a greater impact on Partovi was when Bill Gates left Microsoft, dedicated his life to philanthropy, and created the Bill and

Melinda Gates Foundation, thereby inspiring others to use their wealth for the common good. "It felt to me natural that this was the course I would take." His ideas about education and computer science had gestated for years: he remembered asking Harvard deans about why computer science was not part of the core curriculum. He asked similar questions again in the 2000s while working at different start-ups, where he was always asked to help recruit top talent.

Partovi realized there was a great mismatch in education between the best career opportunities and the availability of quality education in that area. "You'd think the best opportunities would have the most educational supports, that we'd have the most schooling to get people in the most attractive, highest-paying jobs." While Partovi does not want everyone to become a coder, he wants everyone to be exposed to learning the basics of computer science so they can then decide if they wish to pursue it. It is too late to discover coding once you leave high school. Partovi believes coding should be treated the same as learning math and to read and write, because every job today requires some basic understanding of technology, whether you plan to be an athlete, artist, a musician, or a doctor.

Seeding a Talent Movement

Sitting around a firepit with Jack Dorsey, the cofounder of Twitter, and Drew Houston of Dropbox at the Allen and Co. conference in Aspen in 2012, Partovi was asked what he was up to these days. He remembers his honest answer should have been, "Nothing, just hanging out." Unable to offer this answer, he said, "I am starting a new project that will have the best people in tech talk about the importance of computer science education, and in fact, I would love if you both would be part of the video." Partovi had been thinking about doing such a video with Steve Jobs, Bill Gates, and Mark Zuckerberg, with each talking about the power of learning how to program a computer. Steve Jobs's passing prompted him to act as he realized he had lost his opportunity to interview Jobs.

This initial conversation with Dorsey and Houston led to Partovi signing up Bill Gates, Mark Zuckerberg, the basketball player Chris Bosh, well-known artists, musicians, and other successful individuals representing gender and ethnic diversity. This video has been viewed by more than ten million people around the world. Tens of thousands of teachers reached out after viewing the video, wanting to learn more. The small group of people who had produced the video, however, had disbanded after congratulating themselves on the launch.

Then came a request for a meeting with President Obama at the White House. Though overwhelmed, Partovi had to figure out next steps. The video had ten million views in a week, and twenty thousand teachers had written, requesting help in offering computer science at their schools. How could he serve them?

His next moment of inspiration was designing the "Hour of Code," a defining moment in Code.org's history. An idea had just clicked: "This is the best idea I've ever had," he says. When visiting the White House, he asked the president's staff if he could get him to write a line of code—an important way to demonstrate even the president of the United States is not beyond learning computer science. After getting a maybe from the White House, Partovi timed the "Hour of Code" to coincide with the computer science education week, celebrated the first week of December every year. The Hour of Code was launched with President Obama doing a video speech; a year later, President Obama wrote a line of code. Big tech companies lent support and platforms, and Apple and Microsoft stores also held the Hour of Code. Google promoted the Hour of Code on their homepage, and the twenty thousand teachers who had reached out to Partovi signed up to host an Hour of Code in their classroom.

In the seven years since Hour of Code's launch, fifty million students and one million teachers have created ninety million projects, with 49 percent girls and 51 percent boys participating.[17] One of Partovi's goals was to move computer science from being a rich white boys club to an inclusive opportunity for every child around the world.

Creating a Social Movement

Code.org is now one part social movement and one part online learning platform. The social movement component is to change policies, so computer science is available in every school and so that every student has some exposure to it. This is accomplished by changing hearts and minds, from individual parents and teachers to education ministers and heads of state.

During the span of seven years, Code.org has been a part of changing policies in fifty states, including the District of Columbia. Thirty-five countries have announced national plans for computer science. Their online platform is now used by 40 percent of all students in the United States, and the majority of these students are young women and students of color. In a field dominated by white men, this enormous progress has the potential to change the face of computing. According to Partovi, "Our platform is the most popular way computer science is taught."

Partovi's biggest challenge is translating his start-up leadership skills to leading a movement—two very different skill sets. One is leading a company, and the other is leading people. In a moment of self-reflection, Partovi was hopeful he could grow enough to not make too many mistakes along the way. Leading a movement is not measured by how much money Code.org has raised or by how many students use their platform. It is about supporting and inspiring the thousands of other start-ups and non-profits working in the same space so they can continue to grow. It is about the balance between inspiring others and making it about *their* work rather than *our* work, he says. "I still have to learn how to do that better." He says the strongest movement will happen when he is able to disappear and the work continues at the same pace. Movements are not driven by leaders—they are driven by people who believe in an idea and continue to drive the movement forward.

CHAPTER SIX

The Most Good You Can Do

E ffective altruism is a philosophy and social movement that encourages the use of evidence and reasoning to determine the most effective ways to benefit others. In his short but powerful book *The Life You Can Save*, Peter Singer argues that people have a moral imperative to participate in helping the poor. Singer personally gives a third of his income to charity and encourages others to do so.[1] Singer is also a proponent of the effective altruism movement, which uses cost-effectiveness as one of its metrics of measurement of various philanthropic interventions. Raj Kumar in *The Business of Changing the World* contends that it "is impossible to do the calculations on the cost-effectiveness of various philanthropic interventions without making a value judgment about human lives, for example saving the life of a child versus the life of an elderly person."[2]

GiveWell is a website that reflects an effective-altruism ethos and recommends specific charities based on how well they perform. Facebook cofounder Dustin Moskovitz and his wife, Cari Tuna, are strong supporters of GiveWell and of the effective-altruism movement. I have many friends who believe in this approach of making money and then investing in causes that can do the most good based on cost-effectiveness. This always leads to a conversation about how investing in India is cheaper because it is much more cost-effective, that the dollar goes further than when investing in a similar cause in the US.

The focus on evidence and results is important. It has pushed the field of philanthropy and the global aid industry, long focused on good intentions, in the right direction. But one has to be careful and balanced in the approach to doing the most good.

Shankar Vedantam, the host of National Public Radio's weekly show *Hidden Brain*, spoke recently in Seattle at a local nonprofit, Plymouth Housing, which focuses on homelessness in Seattle. There, he shared that each of us can do good things if we allow ourselves to see any problem through the lens of humanity, as opposed to the lens of statistics.[3] David Brooks makes a similar argument in *The Second Mountain*, where he writes that the lens of humanity changes our approach and can become energizing rather than depressing.

In my travels around the world, I have visited countless communities that have challenging living situations. I have never shied away from becoming part of a community, even for a short while. It is important to view every individual through the lens of humanity, as it is only by *tasting the ground one walks on*—immersing oneself in the culture and context of that community—that one can then begin to develop empathy and a sense of purpose. It is only through a deep understanding of the community in which one works that you drive lasting, positive change. The individuals profiled in this chapter are doing that. Three of them left their jobs and uprooted themselves from Seattle to work within the communities they wanted to support. The other two continue their full-time jobs but are effectively using both their humanity and data lenses to ensure their efforts result in the most good for society.

The Ones Who Walk Away

The West African nation of Ghana has had a tumultuous history since gaining independence from the British in 1957: they had a series of alternating military and civilian governments and have finally becoming a stable democratic African nation that is a model for other countries. During the military dictatorship, many Ghanaians migrated either to the UK or the US, fueling a frightening brain drain.

Patrick Awuah was one of those who escaped the military dictatorship in 1985 and came to the United States to study computer science at Swarthmore College. He was one of the few lucky ones, he says. Just 5 percent of college-aged Ghanaians go to college.[4] In 1989, Microsoft recruited him as a program manager. He worked on several projects supporting networking, interconnectivity, and remote access systems, eventually working on the Windows team. He settled in Seattle, married an American, and started a family, leaving Ghana behind. Recounting his visit to Ghana for the first time in five years, he said: "I was extremely disillusioned. Nothing worked. I came back to the US and told my colleagues at Microsoft I would never return to Africa to live."[5]

At Microsoft, he kept his head down and participated at a modest level in the employee giving campaign. In 1994, however, his life was shaken up by the Rwandan crisis. The then head of human resources, Mike Murray, launched a campaign to raise money to support victims, and Awuah donated to that effort. "I remember feeling extremely guilty because here was an American, not an African, who was doing something about a crisis that I had not even thought to get engaged in," he says. At around the same time, his son's birth, coupled with Rwanda and Somalia news headlines, made him think about returning to the continent to help turn things around economically and to help in other ways. "When I looked for the first time into my son's eyes, I realized I had been extremely arrogant to think that I had within me the power to disown a continent," he says. "Africa will matter to my children, to the way they see themselves, the way the world sees them."

The High Risk of Failure

With his wife Rebecca's support, Awuah quit Microsoft and began focusing on how he could return to support the economic development of his country and the continent. Awuah would often wonder if he had done the right thing, as he was afraid of being a failure. He wanted to start something in IT given his professional background, so he traveled to Ghana to observe what was happening at universities and how he could tap into that talent pool. He discovered that students learned programming by writing code by hand on paper and on whiteboards—there were no computers. He realized he could not start an IT company in that environment, without a trained talent pool.

Awuah continued to research these challenges, digging deeper despite receiving contradictory answers to his many questions. These questions and answers eventually converged around a leadership theme. With just 5 percent of college-aged Ghanaians attending university, Awuah understood that current college students would eventually run Ghana's courts, schools, or hospitals, they would design its roads and infrastructure, and they would set financial or environmental policy. Therefore, his calling was to change the structure of Ghana's approach to university learning, to "move it from rote learning, which is a very didactic and authoritarian approach, to a model of critical thinking and problem-solving." He wanted to set an example for other universities by building a curriculum and an ethos that valued and promoted an ethical philosophy and ethical thinking. "And once we are able to change the way the future leaders are educated, you fast-forward twenty to thirty years [and] you['ve] change[d] the leadership of a country." Awuah was inspired by the words of Goethe, "Whatever you can do or dream you can, begin it. Boldness has genius, power, and magic in it—begin it now."[6]

Creating Future Leaders

Awuah did not return to Ghana immediately, enrolling instead in the UC Berkeley's MBA program to understand how organizations worked. Awuah also leveraged the brain trust of his class by including his plans in a class research project.

Awuah was keen to build a university that blended science and technology with the liberal arts in a country without a history of such institutions.

His time at Berkeley also resulted in a long-term collaboration with one of his peers as his business partner. Awuah said it was important to bring on a cofounder, "so you are not in this journey alone, which has been at times very hard." He also recruited Swarthmore College and UC Berkeley to help him codesign the curriculum, which combined elements of a traditional liberal arts college with technical majors.

To ensure that he would be successful, he returned to Seattle to establish the Ashesi Foundation (translates to "beginning"), an organization that would act as the fundraising and evangelism arm for the creation of the university. He tapped into his network of former colleagues at Microsoft to support this effort. Mike Murray was the first to join Awuah and his wife to make a significant contribution to the launch. He invited people not only to contribute but also to join the board of trustees to help with strategic planning, fundraising, and creating awareness. Over the years, a significant number of Microsoft and ex-Microsoft executives have played a role in supporting Ashesi's growth.

In Ghana, Awuah and his colleagues pulled together an advisory board comprising twenty-five faculty members from three universities to help design the curriculum and help with the accreditation process. "It took a year to convince the local accreditation board that a radically different curriculum was valid, and we started classes in March 2002," he says. They started with thirty students in a small building in the capital city of Accra. The initial years were very difficult because they bet on persuading foundations to support their work once they had already started. But most foundations were not focused on higher education in Africa. The UN's Millennium Goals, and now the Sustainable Development Goals, focus on primary education as the metric for country progress.

In 2003, I visited Ashesi to give a talk and interact with students. I was impressed by what Awuah had been able to achieve. In fact, Craig Smith of Digital Partners Foundation and I accompanied Awuah to visit the Kellogg Foundation, with the hope Kellogg would be interested in this innovative approach. When I became head of the philanthropy program at Microsoft, we were unable to lend any support as our funding was restricted to nonformal training centers. But Microsoft employees have continued to support the university and take advantage of the Microsoft match.

The early years were difficult: the dot-com bubble had burst, but a small group of committed donors kept Ashesi's doors open. In 2005, Patrick saw the tide turn when a group of donors pledged enough funding to cover four years of operating costs. On the higher education front, Ashesi University was doing very well. "By the time we graduated our first students in December 2005, Ashesi had become recognized as one of the top universities in Ghana," Awuah says. In 2007, the president of Ghana awarded Awuah the Order of Volta, a national honor.

Expanding the Reach

UC Berkeley business school students had visited on three separate occasions to measure the quality of their brand and the perception of the institute. In just four years, Ashesi had produced remarkable results through its quality educational program and strong students. In 2007, the board's increasing confidence in their growth led them to raise money to build a permanent campus. Their timing coincided with the financial crisis the following year, however, putting them in a challenging place for fundraising. Nevertheless, Awuah recounts that "the remarkable thing was that all the people who had pledged funds for the new campus made good on their pledges, even in the midst of the financial crisis and even though their own personal net worth had declined significantly."

With additional debt financing from the International Financial Corporation, financing was in place to build the campus. Ashesi University is located on a vibrant campus set on a hundred acres in Berekuso, an hour's drive from Accra. The campus currently enrolls twelve hundred students, with plans for further growth. "Fourteen cohorts have graduated to date, which is gratifying and rewarding to see," Awuah says. The placement rate for their students is 95 percent within six months of completing their national service. One in ten of Ashesi alumni have started a business. Some alumni are in financial technology services, and some are in the education and social sector, so Awuah feels satisfied by Ashesi's alumni impact. "We have an alumnus who heads the treasury department of a private bank in Sierra Leone. One is heading a peacekeeping squad in Liberia. One of their alumni was a project engineer developing a biometric registry system for elections, which led to the cleanest elections ever. We have alumni in prominent jobs in the financial technology sector, running orphanages and taking up other incredible positions. I didn't think it would happen this quickly. My heart is filled by this."

Awuah's occupation with systemic change led to a three-year pilot called the Education Collaborative. Other universities have been invited to join in workshops to share curriculum and pedagogy so a network of like-minded institutions can exert leadership in order to transform African leadership on the continent. "It's one thing to build a really great organization," Awuah says. "It's another thing to have an organization that is influencing other organizations in a profound way. We are spending a lot more time thinking about how we make change at a systemic level."

Awuah wants others to benefit from lessons learned. First, he notes that imagining something is just the start; one must take steps to achieve it, so taking steps is the most important thing. "When you envision something, let it really occupy your mind. That really helps guide you." The second lesson is to surround yourself with partners, as the early stages are always challenging. "Having a cofounder was critical so we could help each other. So if you try something big, don't go it alone." The third lesson is the value of fostering good professional relationships, something Awuah has been able to leverage for building and growing Ashesi. The fourth lesson, one he learned from Microsoft, is persistence—keep moving even through hard times.

A Million at Your Doorstep

Growing up in Bangladesh, Tazin Shadid was exposed to altruism early on in life. He became a Boy Scout leader, and his teachers at St. Joseph, a school run by missionaries, were driven by an altruistic mindset. This mindset still drives Tazin today. He says his family's involvement in community also served as "a big catalyst for me—having a mindset of getting involved and helping out communities." Shadid's altruistic mindset mirrors the shift from growth to purpose, a path from *me* to *we*.

Like Awuah, he was fortunate to study in the United States as an undergraduate. After completing his master's in human–computer interactions, HCI, Shadid planned to enroll in a PhD program with ambitions of becoming a researcher specializing in human–computer interaction. His plans were derailed, however, by his department chair, who wanted him to first have some industry experience before joining the PhD program. He joined Microsoft as a vendor and observed the employee giving campaign during his first year there. Though he could not participate, he was amazed at how many employees did and how the campaign created a fun, motivating environment. Soon after, in 2006, he joined Microsoft as a full-time employee and stayed there for a decade.

Health Care as a Gateway

While growing up in Bangladesh, Shadid had been concerned about health care access, given the number of people living in Dhaka's urban slums with no access to services. A mobile health clinic idea appealed to him, especially because he could take advantage of the Microsoft employee giving campaign and leverage it to motivate colleagues to support his idea. He convinced Distressed Children International, an organization he was already supporting, to start a mobile health clinic, even though this was not their area of interest. Shadid agreed to manage the program, and after three years they had evolved the mobile clinic into a fixed clinic.

Using his expertise as a user-researcher at Microsoft, he interviewed people on the ground on his annual visits to Bangladesh. After spending a month there, he designed an approach more comprehensive than just a mobile health clinic. Health care costs were relatively cheap, and he could hire a doctor and nurse and rent a small space to launch the effort. He added up his volunteer time to take advantage of the Microsoft employee match, and he gained support from colleagues and friends. Over the first couple of years, they raised $15,000 to $20,000.

During the first year, Shadid realized that many clinic patients had preventable diseases. So they moved to the next phase of the effort by starting a door-to-door awareness campaign in the slum where the clinic was located. By the third year, they had helped twenty thousand people. But by year five, they realized that health care alone would not solve the poverty problems in these communities. They developed a three-pronged approach to focus on health, education, and skills training. "These three pillars will ensure that a baby is born safely, we can get her or him educated, and we can bring them into the mainstream through skills training and break the cycle of poverty," said Shadid. To develop this comprehensive program, Shadid needed a new approach and a new set of partners. DCI was not interested in scaling the clinics, as these activities were outside their core program competencies. Shadid had a hard choice to make if he was to continue his efforts to deliver additional health care and other services.

Hope, Intention, and Desire

Shadid's vision to fight poverty in Dhaka and Bangladesh needed a new organization, so Spreeha (meaning "zeal"), was born as a nonprofit organization registered in Washington State. Here, again, Shadid tapped into his Microsoft network: one of his colleagues helped file the paperwork and donated the registration fees. In 2012, Spreeha Foundation became a registered nonprofit organization "to empower underprivileged communities to break the cycle of poverty." All through this time, Shadid continued working at Microsoft, and his career thrived as he moved into a leadership role.

One of Shadid's mentors at Microsoft discussed his life goals instead of career goals. She led Shadid through a series of exercises to help him see how to achieve his life goals. "I was very happy at Microsoft, but my ultimate goal was to spend more time at Spreeha and then run it full-time." He worked with his mentor to develop a plan to leverage Microsoft so he could build his skills to be able to leave and run a nonprofit organization effectively. He had research and engineering skills but needed to develop his business acumen, so he moved into a project manager role. Finally, he gained some consumer experience by working at Bing. All these experiences gave him the tools he needed.

Shadid was methodical in his approach: he worked until six or seven in the evening on Microsoft projects and then worked on Spreeha at night when offices opened in Bangladesh. This did take a toll on his personal life. But Shadid had received consistent advice to wait for a few more years to build up Spreeha as an organization before taking the leap to full-time, especially because he could leverage resources available through the employee giving program.

As Spreeha continued to grow, it became clear to Shadid that he would have to make the decision to leave and return to Bangladesh—he now had a staff of seventy people helping eighty thousand individuals in Dhaka. One of his friends, who was also a board member, told him he would need to stop running the organization remotely if he wanted it to work.

Taking the Leap

Leaving a well-paying job is not easy, nor is returning to a place you have been away from for a long time. Having communicated with several Microsoft alumni who had made this leap, Shadid knew he would have to plan carefully, even though he says he had always been a risk taker. Despite his careful plans, he underestimated how much it could cost. Bangladesh had become expensive; for a while, he says, he felt "in a free fall and that I needed to learn to start flying." He also needed to make changes once he realized how to run it more efficiently.

Now part of the system and not just a volunteer, Shadid had to figure out how to take a salary, even though the organization was not large enough to pay him. The people's needs in Bangladesh had evolved, so he explored other opportunities for Spreeha to provide value and to make the organization sustainable. Coming from a corporate background, he was not the typical nonprofit leader, so he started exploring how the expertise that Spreeha had developed in health, education, and skills training could be used differently. He says, "We started establishing social enterprises that would run on a commercial model to provide needed assistance and generate revenue at the same time."

Shadid put his growth mindset to work and applied it for a purpose and with an intention to drive societal change. They started pathology lab services for the elderly and disabled people who could not get to a pathology lab by providing home services to collect samples and then bring the lab reports back to the patients. "We kept our costs low and got paid by the labs, so we did not have to charge the consumer," he says. They have introduced several such services as spin-offs but that help support the work that Spreeha still continues to do in the slums of Dhaka. In December 2018, Spreeha crossed the two hundred thousand mark, and they hoped to cross three hundred thousand people served by the end of 2019.

Afshana and Afrin, two girls who were part of Spreeha's education program at the Rayerbazzar slum in Dhaka, are now chasing their dreams of being a photographer and pursuing higher education, respectively. "These two girls were thinking of dropping from school before joining our program, and now one is enrolled for her master's program. This fulfills the mission of the organization," he says, "but also on a personal level, I feel a lot of fulfillment."

Working in the development sector is never a straight line. In 2017, Shadid along with the rest of the world became aware of a new refugee crisis. Eight hundred thousand Rohingya traveled from Myanmar to the border of Bangladesh to seek refuge from persecution in just two to three weeks. Shadid traveled with one of Spreeha's doctors to go to the border to see if they could help. What Shadid and the team saw was beyond comprehension. "A million people coming to your doorstep without any notice. Mile after mile people were just standing—some were setting up tents. There was no food, bathroom facilities, or clothes. They had been walking for ten to twenty days. We were just shocked," he says. They set up a health camp on the spot. "It was a pretty devastating experience. The first day we saw fifty patients, but there were a few thousand waiting to get a minute of the doctor's time." Most of the refugees were women and children as most of the men had been killed; many of the women were rape victims, and many had become pregnant.

Shadid and the team decided they had to come back and set up a health clinic, even though they had no budget. Today, they have two clinics and two schools for the children. It has been more than two years, and the challenge continues to grow and evolve. At the first health camp, they cared for rape victims and pregnant women. Over the next few months, that evolved to women giving birth and dealing with deliveries and newborns. Now, they are in the midst of another crisis. Diseases that were previously eliminated have resurfaced, as many Rohingya were not vaccinated. Diphtheria, which had been eliminated from Bangladesh a long time ago, has returned and spread.

There is no short-term solution to the Rohingya crisis, and despite many international organizations and the United Nations' support, the population has reached more than 1.3 million. Spreeha's program model in the camps remains similar to their other projects: aiming to create a long-lasting positive impact on the Rohingya community through health care, counseling, education, and awareness. The organization is also partnering with other organizations, like the British Council, and training their teachers, providing them leadership skills, training them how to teach better, and how to engage students. More than seven hundred teachers have been trained so far, multiplying their impact across the country.

Shadid wants to reach a million people in the next couple of years. His vision is to go beyond Bangladesh to other countries with similar needs. Spreeha has built its expertise in health care, education, and training. "What makes us different," he says, "is we are embedded in the community. Because of my skills from Microsoft, we take a human-centered approach, and that differentiates us from other organizations. We become part of the community, we become part of their family, and we build a very strong relationship based on trust. That is what drives our work."

Recently, Shadid has taken Mohammed Yunus's approach to creating a world of three zeros (zero poverty, zero unemployment, zero net carbon emissions)[7] and joined YY Ventures, which is investing in social businesses that are creating a world of three zeros and inspiring innovation and entrepreneurship globally.[8] I got this note from Shadid when I congratulated him on his new endeavor: "Life always comes full circle. After Dr. Yunus won the Nobel Peace Prize and was visiting Microsoft, you arranged for a few of us from [the] Bangladesh team to meet him. That meeting became a huge inspiration for me to start Spreeha. And after all these years, I got the opportunity to work with him directly as YY Ventures was established in collaboration with Yunus Centre."

Supporting Twenty Million Kids to Read

Human history is rich with the building and creation of libraries. Every society has had a rich history of organizing collections of documents. In the newly formed United States, James Madison proposed a congressional library in 1783, and the Library of Congress was established in 1800.[9] Philanthropists and businessmen John Passmore Edwards, Henry Tate, and Andrew Carnegie increased the number of public libraries in the late nineteenth century. Carnegie built more than two thousand libraries in the United States, 660 in Britain, and many more in the commonwealth.[10] Just such a community library in the small town of Athens, Pennsylvania, sparked John Wood's love of reading. In a May 2017 Charlie Rose interview, Wood recounted his love for reading and how it eventually launched him on a journey to bring the joy of reading to twenty million kids. "My family was middle class, but we were rich in books. . . . There were always books in our lives—it gave us a chance to learn, read, and explore the world," he says.

Like many other alumni featured in this book, landing a job at Microsoft was a total coincidence. After his graduate studies at the Kellogg School of Northwestern University, Wood worked—unhappily—in commercial banking in Chicago. "I was not cut out to be a banker," he says. An old friend who just happened to be a Microsoft recruiter found out Wood was unhappy. Within a few weeks, Wood flew to Seattle to interview. Wood joined Microsoft in May 1991 and started working on designing and launching a new product called Microsoft Profit. Wood was fortunate to work with people who went on to become senior executives at Microsoft, including two on the Entry Business Unit (EBU) team: Melinda French (Gates), who ran marketing for EBU and was Wood's hiring manager, and Robbie Bach (who later went on to lead the Xbox business and the entertainment division).

Woods's career progressed at Microsoft, and after stints in several different business groups he found himself based in Sydney, as director of marketing for the Asia Pacific (APAC) region. While in Redmond, Wood participated in the employee giving campaign raising funds for local organizations and getting his team engaged.

Wood has been an outdoor person all his life. He has run sixteen marathons, done major treks, and climbed mountains around the world. Through his marathon running, he has raised money for other causes, and in 1994 had a chance to climb Mount Rainier with the renowned Seattle mountaineer Jim Whittaker. It is his love for the outdoors that eventually led to him to his current role where he is doing the most good he can do.

Not a Single Colorful Children's Book

His love for the outdoors drew him to the Himalayas. He took some time off to trek the 175-mile Annapurna Circuit in Nepal—an eighteen-day effort. The trail climbs to an elevation of eighteen thousand feet along the Tibetan border. "It's a really beautiful region, but like many parts of South Asia, the more remote you get, the more rural you get, the more poverty you see," says Wood. On the second day of his trek, he met the headmaster of a little school, high up in the Himalayas in the small village of Bahundanda. The headmaster invited him to visit the school, and Wood was astonished by the dilapidated conditions, dirt floors, and the dark rooms with limited ventilation. The principal opened a locked door, and he peered into a small room, which was the library. There was not a single colorful children's book.

"They had some backpacker castoffs—you know, some novels and things that other backpackers had left behind but they didn't have any children's books," he recalls. "I asked the headmaster why and he said, 'Well, we're too poor to afford education, but until we have education, we're going to always remain poor.' And that just struck me as the cruelest irony. I had won the lottery of life being born in a wealthy country that could afford a public school system that had libraries, where I had parents who encouraged me to read. And here [were] these kids who basically had their fate decided for them. They lost the lottery of life—they were going to be one more generation to grow up living on a dollar a day."

Thankfully, the headmaster was not afraid to say to Wood, "Perhaps, sir, you will someday come back with books." This was Wood's turning point. He felt that "nothing could be cooler than sharing books." On his return to Kathmandu eighteen days later, Wood wrote an email to friends all around the world, including some Microsoft colleagues, asking them to send him their used children's books. After three months, he had an outpouring of donations and had collected more than three thousand books.

In April 1999, Wood returned to Nepal, this time accompanied by his seventy-three-year-old father, who was looking for a retirement project to undertake. With six donkeys carrying three thousand books, they traveled across the Himalayas, visiting five schools to share the books. Wood wanted to ensure more schools could benefit from their book drive. He says, "Even as we visited those five schools, I met other headmasters who had walked three, four, or five hours from their village because they heard someone was coming with books. They came with letters to say, 'I wish to petition you to help my school; my school needs books too.'" Wood realized that three thousand books were not going to be enough, and serving just the five schools was a good start but a drop in the ocean of need.

Upon his return from delivering books in Nepal, Wood's heart pulled in a different direction than his job, even though he now had a demanding job as the director of business development for the greater China region. He contemplated leaving Microsoft to do something different with his life. He could continue to deliver books to schools in need as a hobby or figure out a solution. "The problem is, hobbies don't scale. The only way to scale is to go all in," he says. "Microsoft is a very demanding place, and that is a good thing—every company should be demanding. I did not want Microsoft to change. So I asked Microsoft to let me go."

Wood's dream was to emulate Andrew Carnegie, who opened twenty-five hundred libraries in the United States and Great Britain. Wood wanted to open libraries around the world and eliminate this barrier to literacy. After nine years at Microsoft, Wood left in 1999 to begin a new stage of his career and build out an organization that would provide books to schools in need. Room to Read was born with his cofounders, Dinesh Shrestha (Nepali) and Erin Ganju (an American who formerly worked at Goldman Sachs and Unilever).

Thirty-Eight Thousand Libraries

Though Room to Read has benefited twenty million children worldwide since its founding in 1999, it was unclear in the beginning how the organization would succeed.[11] "I had not made enough money to start a foundation, so I needed to fundraise from the very beginning," Wood says. "We were an unknown brand, and I had lost my status and nice fancy title at Microsoft." Wood quickly had to learn how to fundraise and attract media coverage. With support from friends and colleagues, they raised $35,000 in the first year by having friends host parties that included those participating in the Microsoft employee giving campaign. Wood would speak to a room of anywhere from five to seventy people to raise a few thousand dollars on up to $10,000 or $12,000.

His persistence—and doors opened through his Microsoft connections—helped him and the team through this phase. In his fourth year, they raised more than $1 million. Within five years, Room to Read had opened six operations in Cambodia, Nepal, India, Sri Lanka, Laos, and Vietnam, with Erin Ganju spearheading this effort. (Currently, Room to Read is in eighteen countries.) "When you have a world of unlimited need, you've got to be able to raise the funds needed," Wood says. "I was constantly on airplanes going to London, to Sydney, to Hong Kong, Singapore, Tokyo—you name it. We started fundraising chapters all over the world."

Wood mastered the art of throwing after-work cocktail parties, generally hosted by a volunteer. His model was simple and transparent: he created a direct causal link between what people gave and what Room to Read did. For example, he would make a pitch that, for $5,000, you can support a library, or for $20,000, you can support the construction of a couple of classrooms. Every six months, the organization would send pictures of what happened with donors' money, along with pictures of the kids and the school or library that was funded. "And that's just how we took off," Wood says. "By 2008 or 2009, we were raising about $12 to $15 million a year, which blew me away. This year we'll raise about $60 million. It's just grown way beyond my wildest dreams. What's important to me is: fundraising is not important for the sake of fundraising itself. Fundraising only matters if you're using the money to do good things." Room to Read has raised a total of more than $600 million, and recently raised $2.1 million in one night at a wine gala in London.

Wood was the face of the organization as he constantly reached out to people, making connections through sheer determination and some luck. He secured early funding from well-known investors, including Marc Andresen (founder of Netscape), Bill Draper and Robin Richards (Draper Richards investment firm), Jeff Skoll (founding president of eBay), and from the family foundation of Don Valentine, the founder of Sequoia. Wood also met with Melinda Gates, whom he had briefly worked for at Microsoft. Gates funded a five-year effort to develop qualitative evidence of transformation taking place through a monitoring and evaluation program. Room to Read now uses this kind of data to improve program quality. "We consider transparency central to our success," Wood says. "This includes developing rigorous methods for determining results through regular data collection against key indicators at more than thirty-five hundred sites annually."

Partnership for Purpose

As much as Wood became the face of the organization, the other two partners were ensuring the success of the projects. Coinvestment became the key for Room to Read to succeed. Local communities coinvest through sweat equity and labor for each project. Government also coinvests alongside Room to Read. The organization in each country is staffed by local people who have the right local knowledge and connections to get things done. More than 90 percent of their workforce consists of local nationals. "We are not dropping into a community and treating them as passive aid recipients; we require the community to coinvest in each project. In other words, we can't want it more than they want it. We can only help you if you want to help yourself," says Wood.

Since they are working in schools, they need the support of the ministries of education, which takes time to develop. Room to Read's strong local connections and staff help with these negotiations, resulting in great partnerships with governments in every place they work. Not a single penny is spent on teacher or librarian salaries—that is all supported locally through the community or through governments. "If the government does not believe enough in the project, we will simply walk away," Wood says. "Thankfully, we haven't had to walk away very often."

Another Room to Read local partnership involves self-publishing books in the local mother tongue. This is important as most for-profit publishers don't publish books in local languages spoken by poor people. So far, they have printed and distributed about twenty-five million books. "We have, in some ways, emulated Carnegie in getting books in the hands of kids around many parts of the world in the language in which they can learn and educate themselves," Wood says proudly.

When I asked Wood to reflect on the lessons he learned at Microsoft, he replied that the most important lesson was making sure local people are involved in everything. Having worked in the Asia region for Microsoft, he learned not to parachute in from outside to tell people in Thailand, for example, how to solve their problems. Having strong, empowered, local employees and local buy-in have been key to their success. He also believes working at Microsoft helped him develop local branding. "Microsoft was just an amazing company and was front and center in the public mindset in the nineties, and that just helped open doors. People would take my meeting," he says.

The Impatient Optimist

Njideka Harry grew up in a comfortable middle-class family of academics in Nigeria, who instilled in her the importance of knowledge and higher education. Her father was a professor at the University of Ibadan, Nigeria's oldest university, and her mother was a schoolteacher and entrepreneur. Though she grew up surrounded by other children of college professors and educators living on the college campus near Lagos, Harry moved to the United States in 1993 to attend university. The situation in Nigeria was unstable at that time, universities were going on strike, and professors were not getting paid. Harry ended up at the University of Massachusetts, Amherst, as her US-citizen mother moved back to the United States and started her master's in education at Harvard University.

Harry recalls that her primary challenges at university were not cultural or societal but about technology and undertaking effective research. "I was coming from a what I considered an upper-middle-class home, and my parents were educators, but I was coming to a developed country, and I was light-years behind in terms of my exposure to technology and the usefulness of technology," she says. That is when she began to think about the impact of technology. "If I was in that position, how much more far behind are those growing up in rural areas whose parents might not be literate? How can they ever compete for twenty-first-century jobs? How can they ever compete in education and entrepreneurship? Because without access to technology, they don't have access to information," she says. This was the first seedling for what was to become Harry's purpose in life.

After completing her undergraduate degree in finance, she joined General Electric and later Microsoft in 1999, working for the corporate planning and analysis team. As an impatient optimist, she felt a compelling force to give back to the land of her birth. "The way for me to give back was in bridging that digital canyon, that digital divide, so to speak," she says. So, in 2000, she founded the Youth for Technology Foundation and incorporated it in 2001.

Information Is Power

While sitting in her cubicle at Microsoft, an article about an organization Microsoft was supporting in Cambodia caught Harry's eye. A few Microsoft employees had traveled to Cambodia to help build a school, and Microsoft had donated software and books. Inspired by this story, Harry considered whether she could start something similar in Nigeria, where there was also great need.

Using the employee giving campaign and various affinity groups, Harry began approaching some of her colleagues to support her effort. She remembers how challenging it was—the effort did not take off right away. In her third year, she saw some increase in the number of people participating and donating. As Harry watched this increase, she decided it was the right time to leave Microsoft.

While at Microsoft, Harry spent a year at Stanford as a fellow in the Reuters Digital Vision Program, which was designed to bring in aspiring technologists with an interest in creating a program or a platform for a developing country. She met some amazing classmates there, including Megan Smith, who became the chief technology officer for President Obama, and Brij Kothari, founder and CEO of PlanetRead. The time at Stanford afforded Harry to work on the Youth for Technology Foundation, build a network of like-minded social entrepreneurs, and learn from them. Upon returning to Microsoft, she decided that the foundation was where she wanted to focus her energies full-time. "I felt like I needed to do something to change the world and I needed to do it right away," she says. This was a very risky move resigning from Microsoft, as her stock options were underwater in 2005 when she left. She was giving up a salaried position for a world of nothing: "No salary, no health insurance, no large grant that I could tap into," she says.

Harry left Microsoft with just her obsession to change the world through technology and to build the foundation. After almost two decades, she notes the numerous ups and downs of her journey. Youth for Technology Foundation (YTF) has had modest success: 1.8 million youth and women have been served through their program, and 330,000 youth have gone through the YTF academy, a more rigorous program with more than 75 percent of students pursuing STEM-related careers or an IT-related education. YTF now operates in five countries: Nigeria, Kenya, Uganda, Colombia, and the United States. Their expansion into Colombia and Uganda was in partnership with other organizations that provide similar services and use the YTF curriculum.

Convincing people to support technology education for underserved communities is a difficult task. I know this from experience running the Digital Partners Foundation and through my work at Microsoft. Most people look at you and say, "Why? There is an education crisis. There are health and sanitation needs, so why focus on technology?" Harry faced the same problem as she went knocking on doors of companies and foundations to support her vision. But Harry believes the key to gaining support was her foresight and focused approach of using youth unemployment and technology data to show the success of their work. Eventually, the communities and her clients spoke on their own behalf and continue to be their own brand ambassadors.

Innovating through Disruptive Technologies

As providing technology to underserved communities became an increasingly crowded field, Harry and her board began to differentiate their work. In 2014, they introduced disruptive technologies into their curriculum, including 3D printing and human-centered design. Harry recalls sitting with private sector leaders at General Electric in Lagos, Nigeria, to explain her vision for entering the 3D printing market and to teach young people how to create, invent, and design the world they envision—to bridge the world of design and manufacturing. "I got blank stares," she says. "Engineers at GE had not seen a 3D printing machine, and you want to bring 3D printing machines to rural and semiurban schools? But today, there are six or seven social enterprises in Nigeria alone implementing 3D printing into their curriculum, though YTF will always be the first to enter the market and deliver value."

Harry told me the story of YTF graduate Amina, also a graduate of biomedical engineering from one of the local universities and a program called 3D Africa. In 2018, she participated in a Hack for Good program that YTF organizes. Her work through the YTF program was recognized at the national level, and she was invited to spend two weeks in Belgium working with other entrepreneurs there. Amina's story illustrates Harry's belief about creating the space for opportunities in technology, especially for girls and women. "Talent is relative, but opportunity isn't," she says.

Radical Transparency

Though Harry's success has not been a linear path, she has embraced radical transparency throughout her journey. This has helped her navigate the ups and downs of being a social entrepreneur. When the organization was still in its nascent phase, it was always hard to be completely transparent with funders about the organization's struggles to make ends meet or to effectively measure impact. Over time, however, Harry's notion of radical transparency has ensured that goals are aligned from the beginning. For YTF, goal alignment means the funder ultimately shares the organization's vision, their ways of measuring success, and their willingness to work alongside YTF. "I don't know all the answers, but I'm very quick up front with being able to identify if a partner's goal is aligned with us and either move on with a partnership or respectfully decline," Harry says. Foundations have approached YTF with requests to work in certain countries, but unless YTF sees complete alignment with its mission, it has respectfully declined the funding, especially if there are any stipulations that might hamper YTF's future work or success.

Over the last several years, YTF has built strong partnerships with companies such as Mastercard, Intel, Uber, Autodesk, and Hewlett-Packard. The private sector is a vital and integral partner when training youth, women, and girls for the work of the future. Each of these companies is involved in YTF's work: employees volunteer in classrooms and have cocreated content. These deep partnerships help them better serve their clients.

Another key lesson that has driven Harry—one learned at Microsoft—is the importance of focus. "There is a lot of noise and distractions out there. I just remember at Microsoft working those seventeen- to eighteen-hour days and really having to be focused surrounded by very smart people," she says. Harry seeks people who are willing to take the initiative, are solution seekers, and are constantly looking to improve themselves. "These are folks that are not waiting for the government or the private sector to bring the learning to their doorstep," she says.

The second key lesson from Microsoft was resiliency. Starting a nonprofit is not easy, and unlike Wood, who was able to tap into the Silicon Valley network, Harry had a difficult time raising funds. But she never gave up and kept true to her core value of not just chasing funding but building deep partnerships. She has proved time and again that she can overcome barriers and keep going; she is constantly adapting and addressing the changes that come her way. Harry has gained recognition for her work: in 2013, she was named a fellow by the World Economic Forum Schwab Foundation for Social Entrepreneurship.

When I asked Harry to reflect on the meaning of purpose, she offered a Muhammad Ali quote: "Service to others is the rent you pay for your room here on earth." For Harry, this means servant leadership and changing the world by doing right. In the social sector, it is not about the salaries but about being on the front lines of the most important work to extend benefits to humanity. A purpose mindset is all about taking risks. "We do not always have the answers going into our work, but our ability to take risks and be flexible is a huge factor," she says. "I consider myself to be a solution seeker." Harry is creating systemic change that will eventually negate the need for YTF as an organization. She hopes a paradigm shift will occur in the philanthropy sector where funders will attend to the well-being of their grantees, so people like her can continue to pay their rent for their time on earth.

Being a Good Mirror

I met Roberto D'Angelo and Francesca Fedeli in the summer of 2014, just as I was about to leave Microsoft. D'Angelo worked at Microsoft in Italy and was in Redmond to participate in the hackathon that had been launched by the new CEO, Satya Nadella. Even though I was leaving Microsoft, their story compelled me to meet them. Over drinks, I learned how they became role models for other parents who have children with disabilities. I choose to end the profiles of changemakers with a purpose mindset through the eyes of D'Angelo and Fedeli's work. The couple has embraced the lessons I want to impart and brings us full circle to illustrate how Microsoft has provided opportunities for employees to become agents of change and a force for good.

D'Angelo and Fedeli were looking forward to the birth of their child in January 2011, after two miscarriages, and they celebrated the birth of their son, Mario, on January 13, 2011. Though it was a premature birth, all signs showed Mario was healthy. In Italy at that time, infants born prematurely were part of a brain scan pilot program, the results of which showed that Mario had suffered a perinatal stroke and 40 to 45 percent of his right hemisphere had been damaged; his right hemisphere neurons had disappeared and could never be replaced. This was devastating for them, as it would be for any parents. "We thought we were prepared for life with a newborn, but we were not ready for this. Like many parents of children with needs outside of 'normal,' we found no owner's manual that answered the millions of questions we had or that had advice on what to do next," says D'Angelo.

For three years, they scrambled to adjust. Without an owner's manual, they did everything they could to treat Mario's cerebral palsy and epilepsy. They started physiotherapy and rehabilitation and were then introduced to the concept of "mirror neurons" developed by Giacomo Rizzolatti from the University of Parma. "The basic theory of mirror neurons simply says that if you watch someone else slowly grab an object (with purpose) it will activate the exact same neurons in your brain as if you were performing the action. And the 'action observation treatment' derived by this theory seemed to be the leading edge in motor skills rehabilitation," says D'Angelo.

Mirror Neurons

D'Angelo and Fedeli started showing Mario how to grab objects. One day, they noticed that Mario was not looking at their hands but at their faces. "In our faces, he saw that we were sad, we were depressed, and we were looking at him as a problem, not our son in a positive light. That moment really changed our perspective," says D'Angelo.

They began developing a long-term plan for Mario and a support network for parents in similar situations. They discovered that early intervention is key to gaining ground and stimulating neuroplasticity. In his 2017 *Medium* article "Consider What You Have as a Gift and What You Lack as an Opportunity," D'Angelo writes that "the more we researched, the more we found that 'everyone' had their own reasons to avoid the management and treatment of messy brain damage. For investors, 3.5 million kids are not a profitable market; for scientists, the brain of a kid is by far more complicated than the brain of an adult (that by itself is one of the most complex things in the universe); for the pharma industry these kids could have remained impaired all life long, they're not taking any kind of pills for their health status. Everyone had an excuse for not doing more. In the end, we supposed it's because it's not their child."[12]

An invitation from TED Conferences to speak at the TED GLOBAL 2013 event in Edinburgh gave them an opportunity to share their experience for the first time. Their simple message was that "we realized that what Mario has is a gift and what he misses is just an opportunity for improvements. And we realized that we had to become a better 'mirror' for Mario. We stopped to look at him as a problem and we started to look at him as a son. We stopped to focus on what was not working and we focused on what was working and build on his strengths. And as he became stronger on his right side, the left side (impacted by the stroke) started to follow and improve." This was a brave step for them to share their experience with more than a million people via video. But after speaking at the TED conference, they were inundated with requests for advice from parents in similar situations. This then gave them the courage to do more. In 2014, they also understood that the best way to help their son was to help every kid in the world like him and they founded FightTheStroke, a nonprofit advocating for young stroke survivors.

D'Angelo and Fedeli began collaborating with Rizzolatti and other brain experts from around the world, dreaming of creating a platform where children could learn from other children through technology and parents and doctors could get help. In 2015, a chance meeting with Satya Nadella gave them hope and changed their perspective. Nadella was aware of their work since he also has a son with cerebral palsy. He introduced D'Angelo to Jenny Lay-Flurrie (who works on accessibility) and Tim Allen (who leads the inclusive design team). "Their perspectives on inclusive design and how technology could help us with the challenges faced by our family, our nonprofit, and our growing social enterprise both inspired me and renewed my confidence in our vision: to transform ourselves into changemakers and to create a platform that reshapes the problem of a few into an opportunity for many," says D'Angelo.

The Three Elephants in the Room

D'Angelo and Fedeli were working on three big issues. First, they discovered that parents who have children with disabilities did not have a support network, and so they set out to build a platform that connected parents via an online support group. Today, it is one of the largest such networks in Italy and collaborates with other networks around the world.

The second issue was effective physiotherapy and rehabilitation. D'Angelo took time off for nine months to care for his son (as allowed under Italian law) and started work on Mirrorable, a motor-skills rehabilitation platform that uses technology and toolkits to promote learning while observing, directly in partnership with Professor Rizzolatti's mirror neuron's scientific staff.[13] The initial support for Mirrorable came through a Hack for Good that D'Angelo participated in with a team of Microsoft employees from around the world. After clinical trials in 2019, several families are now testing the Mirrorable platform.

The third major issue was epilepsy. Most new parents don't get enough sleep. But for D'Angelo and Fedeli, they had the additional challenge of keeping watch over Mario in case he had a seizure at night. In 2019, D'Angelo put together a team of twenty-nine Microsoft employees from around the world. The team had a wide variety of talents: research, development, design, and marketing.[14] They were also people who were disabled, had recovered from a stroke, were cancer survivors, and so forth, each bringing his or her strengths and unique perspectives to develop an end-to-end, scalable proof of concept: MirrorHR—Epilepsy Research Kit for Kids, a mobile app connected to a wearable device that sends alerts when a potential seizure activity is identified and help parents and doctors in having better insight via an innovative AI-based Video Diary feature. The team won the 2019 Microsoft Hackathon Grand Prize.

D'Angelo wants everyone to know that epilepsy is not a challenge you can solve with an app. As a parent, he has been disappointed by numerous programs offering a miracle solution. He understands that parents are counting on him, but he also understands this will be a long, hard road to develop a commercial product. The goal is to reduce the overall number and severity of seizures, thanks to a consumer-grade wearable device that monitors the child and a AI-based way to track potential triggers, so that families can increase their self-management potential while doctors can have more precise data and insights. This means there is a greater chance the family will not have to rush to the hospital and can proactively adjust their behaviors and mitigate the triggers. "What I'm saying is we are doing our best to give you better insights," he says, adding that as everyone works together we can only get better at it. The hackathon team members will continue to use machine learning to help parents and doctors discover what, exactly, triggers the seizures.

Priority with a Purpose

It has been a long and difficult journey for D'Angelo and Fedeli, one in which they had to make major adjustments to their lifestyle, such as significantly reduced work travel. As Fedeli is focused full-time on their nonprofit, D'Angelo is the family's sole provider. They have cut expenses but are happy and very positive. "I work for Microsoft for eleven months, and I am giving back 10 percent of my salary. But for one month, Microsoft is working for me, and that is the beauty of Hack for Good, and that is the beauty of this culture," says D'Angelo. They both work on their foundation and the new social enterprise, but their purpose is very clear. "I will continue on this even if there is only a 1 percent chance of success because I want to be able to tell Mario on his eighteenth birthday that we tried and we found joy and purpose with you beside us," D'Angelo says.

D'Angelo and Fedeli's perspective is what I espouse in this book: they are working to develop Mario's strengths rather than focus on overcoming his weaknesses. And they are bringing the best out of every person, so together they can design an effective solution. D'Angelo has had to continuously evolve his teams and change course when needed. He also had to ensure the team was diverse enough, with each person bringing a specific talent and being willing to work as a team.

What their work shows is the importance of discovering our strengths, understanding our weaknesses, and then embracing our strengths, finding people along the way who complement those strengths and weaknesses. Our lives are not a problem to be solved but a mystery to be embraced. For D'Angelo and Fedeli, Mario is a challenge to be embraced, one that gives them enormous joy and purpose.

CHAPTER SEVEN

Purpose Mindset

The spring of 2020 has given us a rare chance to reflect upon a common challenge and how deeply we are connected to one another. The COVID-19 pandemic compels us to examine our human behavior and to develop resiliency by building healthy, interdependent systems. Bonding, social sanctuary, and authentic connection have become imperative in this time of need. Over the last few months, millions of people have applied their sense of connectedness and shared responsibility, moving the focus from "me" to "we," thereby contributing to our collective well-being. Slowly but surely, we are moving from the survival of self to survival of the community, such as through "physical distancing" and other community-led measures to ensure humankind continues to thrive.

This did not come easy. Mandatory lockdowns have led to draconian measures in some countries, while in others, physical distancing has continued to be lax. Deaths have risen, job loss has been extreme, and displacement continues to unfold, as people struggle to return to their homes or villages. Early on, an individual survival-mode mentality prevailed, as we hoarded basic necessities, such as toilet paper, hand sanitizers, face masks, and food, as a way to assuage our anxieties. We ignored orders to stay inside and practice physical distancing. Even then, we witnessed numerous acts of kindness and altruism from complete strangers for those most impacted or for the frontline workers of the pandemic. We moved from individual survival to collective empathy; we also became adept at working from home and socializing while practicing physical distancing. Strikingly, we have moved rapidly toward compassion and empathy, two ingredients in developing our individual and collective purpose mindset.

The British journalist and author George Monbiot's foretelling of a new political-economic narrative that builds on community rather than on individualism is playing out as we grapple with the pandemic. In *Out of the Wreckage: A New Politics in the Age of Crisis*, he shows how research in the fields of psychology, anthropology, neuroscience, and evolutionary biology converge to reveal human beings' outstanding capacity for altruism, ingrained in our DNA through natural selection. The "politics of belonging" he writes about include creating a more participatory democracy, where many important decisions are made at the local level. His idea of inclusive communities based on "bridging networks" (which bring together people from different backgrounds) rather than "bonding networks" (which bring together people from the same group or community) is central to how humanity interacts and works together.[1] The COVID-19 pandemic created just such an opportunity for people to form new bridging networks to help their communities build on altruism and cooperation.

The 100 Million Mask Challenge[2] is an excellent example of how bridging networks sprung up to help health care professionals secure medical-grade personal protective equipment, which was in short supply due to global demand. The challenge, initiated by the Providence Group of hospitals, invited the community to participate by sewing protective masks. The organizers distributed kits that included medical-grade, lab-tested material to make one hundred masks each. Shortly after this campaign announcement, hundreds with a willing heart, the ability to sew, and a sewing machine claimed these kits. This overwhelming response continued to grow and morph, enveloping more segments of society in a bridging network designed to make a difference.

Major companies, such as JD.com and Alibaba in China and Amazon and Walmart in the United States, started hiring people who lost their jobs in other industries.[3] Large restaurant chains and food suppliers to restaurants began donating their meals to schools, health care workers, or those in need.[4] As these acts accumulate, communities become closer and foster a sense of hope and purpose.

Samir Bodas, cofounder and CEO of Icertis and a Microsoft alumnus, has also created a bridging network. Icertis recently announced a $50,000 contribution to the Alliance for Education to provide twenty to twenty-five thousand meals to schoolchildren in need. "As our communities take historic steps to protect public health in the face of the COVID-19 global pandemic," he says, "here in the Seattle area, we are beginning to identify and respond to the secondary challenges caused by that response. While critical to slow the spread of the virus, closing schools, businesses, and events [the response] unfortunately creates uncertainty and hardship—especially for economically vulnerable children and families."

One impact has been the closure of schools for six weeks leaving approximately sixty-eight thousand King County children without access to school breakfast and lunch programs. "Shortly after we instituted work-from-home in our Bellevue office, the wife of one of our Icertians, who is a local schoolteacher, identified a first, quick action we could take to contribute to the community response," Bodas says. "She brought it to our attention that during the school year, many economically disadvantaged children receive most of their nutrition at school, and the school closings could have an adverse impact on these children's health and well-being." This was an easy decision for Bodas. The company usually gathers each day to share a company-funded meal, but as the company's employees shifted to remote work, there was no need to buy these meals. The leadership decided to support the community and extend the common good.

Bodas was particularly proud of how the India office, headquartered in Pune, came together quickly to launch their billboard campaign "Let's join hands in namaste," amplifying the Indian prime minister's speech calling for a nationwide curfew. "The team went from zero—PM's speech—to billboards going up across Pune in seventy-two hours flat," he says.

Icertis is one example of the thousands of companies and individuals supporting their communities. Large and small companies instituted work-from-home policies, and in many cases, companies like Microsoft committed to paying all its support staff while the campus was closed. Young Investment Company announced it was forgoing rent for April so restaurants could pay their employees instead.[5]

In the Seattle area, the Seattle Foundation and its CEO, Tony Mestres, launched the COVID-19 response fund, which is a coalition of philanthropy, government, and business partners, to rapidly deploy resources to community-based organizations at the front lines of the outbreak in the Puget Sound region. The initial goal was $10 million, but by March 30, the fund had raised $16 million, and by mid-May, $23 million, including $700,000 in online gifts from more than three thousand individual donors.[6] By the end of March, $10.1 million had already been distributed to 120 nonprofits.

A larger effort launched on March 23, called All in Seattle,[7] raised $27 million in four days and as of this writing some $30 million. Seattle is not the only city with such efforts. Bloomberg Philanthropies, Carnegie Corporation of New York, the Doris Duke Charitable Foundation, and twenty-three other foundations, as well as individual donors, have created a $78 million COVID-19 rescue fund for New York City nonprofits.[8]

These efforts build a collective sense of purpose and create bridging networks to help us find our way out of the COVID-19 pandemic. This collective sense of purpose is the bridge by which complete strangers are coming together for the well-being of humanity. What I hope will happen is that our collective sense of purpose will eventually create a new vocabulary of how we think about the role we all play to extend the common good.

Microsoft Leading the COVID-19 Response

Microsoft has launched a multipronged effort to support and invest in the COVID-19 response. They immediately donated $1 million for the Seattle

Foundation COVID-19 response fund, and many of Microsoft's senior executives have participated in the All in Seattle effort. In addition, to help address the impact of COVID-19 worldwide, the company launched a new Microsoft Give Together Global Employee Giving Campaign. Microsoft Philanthropies implemented a two-month employee global giving program during April and May of 2020, which included the opportunity for each employee to have matched up to $10,000 donated to eligible nonprofits. This match benefit was in addition to any existing match benefits. In three months, the campaign has raised over $42.8 million, which includes a dollar-for-dollar company match to more than ten thousand nonprofits in sixty-nine countries.

The company has developed a multilayered approach, in which it is using its AI technology for virus research, Microsoft stores are delivering emergency remote operations, their health care bots are helping fight against the virus, and the campus dining resources are helping families in need.[9]

Microsoft has also partnered with UNICEF to launch a global learning platform to help children and youth continue their education at home. Learning Passport started off as a partnership between UNICEF, Microsoft, and the University of Cambridge, and it was due for launch later in 2020, but the launch was accelerated to meet the needs of the current crisis.[10]

At the end of June 2020, Microsoft launched an initiative to help twenty-five million people worldwide acquire digital skills that are needed in a COVID-19 economy. Microsoft is providing a range of tools, training, and certifications to millions of people worldwide in multiple languages. In addition, Microsoft has also committed $20 million in financial grants, plus technical support, to nonprofit organizations around the world.[11]

Moving from Passion to Purpose

In my role at Microsoft, I had daily encounters with people who expressed their passion for making a difference. I remain curious about why passion should be a critical component of work, as work is a personal matter, one that benefits the individual more than society. Though we hear we must have a passion for what we do, rarely do we hear the word *purpose*. I, too, exude passion when I discuss my work, but passion alone is just not enough. We must focus on a collective sense of well-being and extending the common good, and for that, we need to develop a sense of purpose and our purpose mindset.

When people wanted to join my team at Microsoft, I didn't ask them how passionate they were about making a difference. Instead, I asked them to share a difference they had made, however small or insignificant it might be. This was a far more insightful way to discover their strengths and purpose. Eleanor Roosevelt's thoughts about life and purpose encapsulate my approach: "The purpose of life is to live it, to taste experience to the utmost, to reach out eagerly and without fear for newer and richer experience."

Purpose implies you are leading from values that will guide you in making the right decisions. Anne Loehr, an expert in preparing leaders for the workforce of the future, states that most people have five to seven core values that each of us demonstrates differently in our daily actions and language. Understanding your values isn't simple; it's a lifetime challenge that requires practice, but our values give us a sense of purpose.[12] Purpose is continuing to become an important driver for companies as I show in the following pages, starting with how our economy is transitioning to a purpose economy.

The Purpose Economy

I asked my friend, Aaron Hurst, for his views on passion. As the author of *The Purpose Economy* and founder of Imperative, a platform connecting and supporting employees as peer coaches, he was the perfect person to ask. Purpose comes first for Hurst. He has built a career around his work on purpose, exemplified by his founding of Taproot Foundation, which engages employees to undertake pro bono service projects to help nonprofits build capacity.

Hurst has worked with many companies to help build their volunteer and pro bono service model. This model involves skills-based volunteering, in which professionals apply their know-how in technology, finance, and HR to help nonprofits build capacity, rather than engaging in traditional volunteering. Bill Neukom, who established Microsoft's employee giving program, also had extensive experience providing pro bono legal services. Hurst built on that model to found Taproot and to expand pro bono efforts to span all fields.

Hurst explains that Taproot was a response to a deeper problem of employees feeling a lack of purpose in their day jobs. "What we had done at Taproot wasn't just about volunteerism; what we'd actually done was tapped into the growing demand in the workplace to help people be more fulfilled in their careers," he says. He left Taproot to start Imperative because he wanted to focus on increasing employees' purpose so that *all work* would feel like pro bono work. In doing so, employees would become more productive. Through Imperative, Hurst supports individuals in identifying what he calls "purpose drivers," the first step to becoming more fulfilled at work. Imperative also connects employees with peer mentors to further increase their sense of purpose and fulfillment at work.

According to Hurst, there is a seismic shift in the world economy, in which consumers, employees, and organizations are becoming interested in their impact on the world around them. This "purpose economy" is built around people's desire for fulfillment. Just as technology became essential to businesses in the 1990s, purpose is becoming essential for both employees and customers today.

One key finding in Hurst's book is survey-based data showing that employees naturally fall into three motivation categories at work. Some people view work as a financial transaction—they need money to pay the bills. Another third sees work as creating an identity and a sense of belonging. "It's about status; the profession defines who I am," says Hurst. The final third is driven by purpose—the work itself is an opportunity to add value to the world and create a sense of fulfillment.

Hurst and his team's studies found that people with a purpose mindset had higher work-performance scores than those in the other two categories. Hurst does not want to force every employee to have a purpose mindset. Instead, he wants to activate purpose as employees' *secondary* driver, creating a culture where everyone can show up as their full selves, including having psychological safety and a sense of belonging. Microsoft's employee giving program offers such a culture, helping every employee—if they so choose—to find ways to show up as their full selves. We must keep in mind, however, that companies must move beyond how purpose helps with recruitment and retention toward how purpose helps companies make our societies better, more resilient, and more sustainable.

Chris Jarvis is the founder of Realized Worth, a global corporate social responsibility consultancy that specializes in employee volunteer training, volunteer program design, and employee engagement. Jarvis offers an important perspective on how companies can lead. Companies already create a sense of identity. For example, a Microsoft employee has a particular social identity versus that of an Apple employee, and that identity holds around the world. This is different from a city, state, or country identity. A company's identity transcends physical and cultural boundaries. In his work, Jarvis finds that, in some ways, a company's culture is more important than a country's culture and it plays an important role in changing employees' behavior.

Hurst's and Jarvis's insights are crucial because they show how employers and decision-makers have an incredible opportunity to model a value system and a set of truths in a way that can radically change people's views of themselves, their belief systems, and their behavior. Therefore, companies around the world have the same opportunity to help employees understand the importance of issues like equity, inclusiveness, and diversity in the workplace. Companies have already demonstrated how well they can promote a growth mindset. Today, the tide is shifting, and purpose is becoming a vital part of employee growth, business impact, and societal impact.

Evolution of the Purpose Economy

This shift toward purpose has been incubating for many years. Since 1983, Carol Cone, one of the pioneers in this field, has supported companies uncover their reason for being, beyond profits—to help them find their purpose. When she started her work, few companies saw the value of aligning with a social issue at their core. Today, Cone sees the need for successful companies/brands to have meaning and relevance to all stakeholders. Wise companies who see purpose as business strategy, not only seek to discover or refine their purpose but also seek its activation, deeply embedding it into their culture, operations, innovation, and society. Today, and even more tomorrow, it matters what a company stands for. This shift has been brought on by the transparency afforded by the internet, consumers' tremendous number of choices, the war for talent, and the evolving views of our relationship with work. "If I'm going to commit myself to work, I want the work to reflect my values," she says. And the shift goes beyond the individual. The biggest shift we are witnessing, that will exponentially drive purpose as business and brand strategy, is the financial community's recognition that purpose driven companies are clearly better managed companies, creating business growth and impact on society.

Larry Fink, the CEO of BlackRock (roughly $6 trillion under management), proclaimed in his 2018 client letter: "Without a sense of purpose no company, either public or private, can achieve its full potential." His 2019 message was even more pointed: "Purpose is not the sole pursuit of profits but the animating force for achieving them. . . . Profits are in no way inconsistent with purpose—in fact, profits and purpose are inextricably linked."[13] Following this trend, the Business Roundtable announced a new Statement on the Purpose of a Corporation in 2019, signed by 181 CEOs who committed to lead their companies for the benefit of all stakeholders—customers, employees, suppliers, communities, and shareholders.[14]

This is a massive shift. Cone and her firm, Carol Cone ON PURPOSE, undertook research in collaboration with Harris Poll and the Association of National Advertisers in 2019 to prove the power of purpose beyond B2C companies and brands. This was Cone's thirtieth piece of research over her career illuminating the power of purpose as business strategy. They surveyed 259 business-to-business professionals, working in companies with revenues ranging from $50 million to $2 billion.[15] Cone was surprised by the results, as 86 percent said purpose was either critical or very important to the growth and future of their business. But a deeper dive found that only 24 percent said purpose is embedded in their business to the point of influencing culture, innovation, operations, and their engagement with society. See Figure 3.

The Stated Purpose vs. Activated Purpose Gap

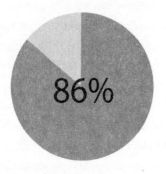
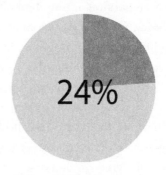

Stated Purpose

Purpose is important to business

Purpose sets a clear "North Star" for
the business, articulating why it exists

Activated Purpose

Purpose is embedded in business

Purpose is activated across the business,
from culture and innovation to operations
and engagement with society

*The B2B Purpose Paradox: How Purpose Powers Business-to-Business
Growth, 2020, Cone On Purpose. Re-created by Ada Gupta—RedAlkemi*

FIGURE 3

"Purpose payoff comes from depth and longevity. Purpose is not a statement that lives on a wall or in a handbook. In action, purpose is both captivating and highly effective across business metrics, from sales to impact on society," says Cone. Employees play central roles in the activation of purpose, so companies must arm them with the knowledge, tools, and resources to embed purpose within the company. Companies have a demonstrated track record of promoting a growth mindset, which happens to be critical in developing a purpose mindset. One needs self-growth to serve both at the company level and then at the community level.

Purpose for Humanity

The year 2020 ushered in a new reality. Business cannot be conducted as usual: this is a time where humanity is reflecting on what we hold dear, how we can shape humanity for the better, and how purpose shapes our mindset. On March 24, 2020, Hubert Joly, the executive chairman of Best Buy, published an article in the *Harvard Business Review* titled "A Time to Lead with Purpose and Humanity."[16] He explores how business leaders are implementing that Business Roundtable statement of purpose, work that is vital now more than ever.

According to Joly, the pandemic is an existential crisis, and the leaders he interviewed are rising to the occasion in the name of humanity with a clear human focus in mind. "This is a time when performance will be judged by how a company and its leadership serve everyone and fulfill a higher purpose—and specifically how they have shown up and met the requirements and expectations of its multiple stakeholders," writes Joly. This chapter relates stories of how small and large companies are rising to this challenge, focusing on purpose and humanity.

Over the last several weeks of the crisis, under Satya Nadella's and Brad Smith's leadership, Microsoft and its employees have further embodied their principle of purpose by launching several initiatives to supply needed health care supplies to hospitals and other medical facilities. In Puget Sound, they are shifting gears to provide thirty thousand boxed lunches for local families in need and to donate 240,000 surgical masks and thirty-five thousand hand sanitizers and additional supplies to Washington State. They are also working with business partners and customers to provide access to Teams (Microsoft's online collaboration tool), so remote working is made possible.[17]

Authenticity is key in activating purpose and implementing it at any company. This requires companies to go beyond creating a tagline or embracing purpose as a driver. It requires effective implementation, which, in turn, demands hard work, tenacity, and long-term planning. Carol Cone talks about the work she and her firm did with Rockport back in the '80s. They completely re-created the purpose of the company as a "walking shoe" company and developed clear metrics to share the benefits of walking (before walking became a trend). They did it to compete as a business, but in doing so they changed the conversation around the benefits of walking by embedding walking as a culture within the company. Every employee got a pair of shoes, was allowed to take a walk at work, and the company built walking trails around their offices. This allowed them to innovate and to tout the benefits of walking, including developing the "Rockport fitness test," which measures an individual's aerobic fitness levels.[18] In this time of crisis, Cone is seeing a renewed sense of purpose among organizations, and she is sharing many of these stories on her podcast,[19] hoping to show others why leading with purpose means leading the world.

The Purpose Generations

Younger generations are coming to work with a new mindset. Many want to work for more than just a paycheck; they want to feel connected to their organization's mission and values. They also want to feel connected to the missions of the brands they buy. Millennials and Gen Zers are the purpose generations.

Millennials and all Gen Zers grew up with the internet and are accustomed to having access to a wealth of information. With access to virtually unlimited information about companies, employers, and social causes, young people are well-informed workers and consumers. This generation is also used to spending a great deal of time at work. The "work-life blend" has come to replace a "work-life balance" as more young people (particularly in "knowledge-based" jobs) are expected to bring work home or spend long hours at their workplaces, which are the basis of their social lives. When work is all-encompassing, finding purpose at work becomes more important. Susan McPherson, CEO of McPherson Consulting, a well-known corporate social responsibility firm, says, "There is no such thing as our work selves and our home selves. We have to find more enhancement in our day jobs because they're not day jobs anymore, and there has to be some other motivation than completing a sale or finishing application code."

Approximately 75 percent of millennials say they are willing to take a pay cut to work for a more responsible company, and 64 percent say they would not join a company without strong CSR values.[20] As companies compete for young talent, particularly in tech- and knowledge-based industries, they can set themselves apart with purpose. Young people want more than just *knowing* their company is doing good. They want to *experience* purpose and giving and are willing to forgo higher pay accordingly. Many also see doing good as a social activity.[21] McPherson reminds me that "companies are made up of people, and people are made up of values, and therefore, companies have to value something."

A noteworthy caveat to this data is that these trends reflect highly educated, knowledge-based workers' preferences, rather than those of lower-paid workers. Lower-income workers do not always have the luxury of finding a job at a value-driven company; their priority is to put food on the table. Likewise, their tight budgets don't always allow for paying more for purpose-oriented brands.

But many of the younger generation are still driven by a sense of purpose in their work and their life. I see that drive in my students, many of whom are first-generation college students. I believe these values will remain with them despite the current economic climate. Young people from all walks of life are being driven by their values and purpose; they are demanding government and business action toward inclusive and equitable policies. Occupy Wall Street, Black Lives Matter, environmental activism, climate change, women's rights, and the Me Too movement have brought out people from all walks of life to become deeply engaged.

From Growth to Purpose Mindset

Our mind is what separates us from all other living creatures. How we use our mind makes a world of difference in what we can achieve. The environment in which we live, the policies that govern us, and the companies we work for all play a role in how we shape and use our mind. The examples of individuals and their journeys that I've shared have given us insights into their opportunities and the mindset they applied in seizing those opportunities.

The world-renowned Stanford University psychologist Carol S. Dweck pioneered the power of mindset and showed how success in areas of human endeavor could be dramatically influenced by how we think about our talents and abilities. Since 1988, her work has shown how a person's mindset prepares them to seek either performance or learning goals. A student with a performance orientation might be worried about looking smart all the time and will, therefore, avoid challenging work. On the other hand, a student with a learning orientation will pursue interesting and challenging tasks in order to learn more. In subsequent studies, Dweck found that people's theories about their own intelligence significantly impacted their motivation, effort, and approach to challenges. Those who believe their abilities can improve are more likely to embrace challenges and persist despite failure. Her model of a fixed versus a growth mindset shows how cognitive and behavioral abilities are linked to one's beliefs about the malleability of their intelligence.

In the updated edition of *Mindset: The New Psychology of Success*, Dweck expands the mindset concept beyond the individual, applying it to the cultures of groups and organizations. But I am arguing that we must go beyond the growth mindset and develop a purpose mindset, which extends beyond an individual or business to benefit all of us. Rich Kaplan, leader of the Microsoft employee experience group and a cancer survivor, has his purpose in finding a cure for cancer. By working with the Fred Hutchinson Cancer Research Center in Seattle, Kaplan is connecting the dots between a growth mindset and a purpose mindset. By encouraging Microsoft employees to lend their expertise and time, he helps the center build data architecture and a network that brings together experts who work on bioanalytics, big data, and the cloud. Kaplan says that although people think Microsoft is a software and hardware company, he does not see it that way: "It's about empowering the world and making the world a better place."

Purposeful Organization

Nadella in his LinkedIn article "Achieving More for the World" states, "As we consider the opportunities and the pressing challenges facing the world today—as we work to empower 7 billion people on the planet—we must recommit to this sense of purpose and mission and redefine what achieving more means for the world."[22] In my interview with Nadella, he went on to say that "companies will have to go beyond being rent seekers to delivering value; 2020 has brought that in sharp focus: When a company does well, who else is doing well? Is the world more sustainable? Is the growth that is being brought about more equitable? Is there more trust because of your institutional strength?" (Rent-seeking activity is often described as "predatory" capitalism winning out over "productive" capitalism.)[23]

Oxford professor Colin Mayer's definition of purpose of a corporation has been the inspiration for Nadella. Mayer writes that the purpose of business is "profitable solutions to problems of people and planet." This approach must become the key driver for companies so they can answer the question "Who else is doing well because we are doing well?"

Raj Sisodia spoke to me about how purpose unleashes creative and caring energy, not just physical energy. He went on to suggest that creating a shared purpose is very important. In their book *Conscious Capitalism*, Sisodia and his coauthor, John Mackey, CEO of Whole Foods Market, show that shared purpose brings together all of the stakeholders, including customers, suppliers, investors, employees, and society. "When you have shared purpose," they write, "your interest aligns for the flourishing of the enterprise in which everyone is connected; so shared purpose is the glue that holds everybody together."

The global average for employee engagement is 18 percent according to Gallup; in the US that number is 33 percent.[24] But Sisodia states that their research has showed a purpose-conscious company will have a 70 percent or more employee engagement, which includes increased conviction and commitment. "You know, ultimately, everything runs on human energy," he says. The same Gallup report also found that disengaged employees cost between $450 and $500 billion to the US economy each year.

Part of the reason is that many working people suspect their job is pointless. In 2018, two Dutch economists did a study of a hundred thousand workers in forty-seven countries. Eight percent found their jobs socially useless, and 17 percent were doubtful about their work's usefulness.[25] Giving opportunities for employees to build their purpose for their work is important, as it can also bring economic benefits to the company. Work has to be a place where all employees feel they are contributing and making a difference. "Ultimately, every business can and should be a place of healing for those that work there and a source of energy rather than a place of suffering," says Sisodia.

Our awareness of inequities is getting higher "and sadly this epidemic, whether it's inequities between countries or within countries, is going to get wider, even if you look at big businesses versus small businesses," Bill Gates says. "You know, in fact, a few companies are thriving and a lot are suffering. The opportunity to step up is pretty dramatic." Every business has a role to play, and many companies are doing their part. But more needs to be done. The Bill and Melinda Gates Foundation is working with both big and small pharma companies to develop vaccines, and according to Gates their response has been great. Gates hopes that this current crisis increases everyone's awareness to the inequities and drives more companies and people to contribute to extend the common good. Jaime Dimon, chief executive of J. P. Morgan, has expressed a similar sentiment in his memo ahead of the bank's shareholders meeting: "It's my fervent hope that we use this crisis as a catalyst to rebuild the economy that creates and sustains opportunity for dramatically more people, especially those that have been left behind for too long."[26]

Purpose Mindset

As a global community, we have become reasonably adept at describing the need for change "out there" in the world, such as promoting social justice and combating climate change. But we are not so good at talking about the change that also needs to happen within us. What shifts in our beliefs, attitudes, and assumptions are necessary to bring out the best in ourselves and to do good? The purpose mindset framework is a simple yet sophisticated framework for exploring the shifts that can take place within our inner selves.

What sets purpose leaders apart from their fixed- and growth-mindset counterparts is their aspiration to discover their strengths so they can meaningfully contribute to causes greater than the self. They question *why* they do what they do and believe in creating a good, just, and equitable society. Jens Molbak has spent most of his life as an entrepreneur and successful businessman; at age twenty-six, he founded Coinstar, the coin-collecting machines in grocery stores. I have known Molbak for several years because of his recent work around creating trisector business models where the public, private, and social sectors come together to deliver solutions at scale to improve people's lives.[27]

I spoke to Molbak about the business-model transition he is witnessing and why purpose has become such an important issue. Molbak's immigrant family from Denmark instilled in him the belief that business, government, and the community must bring value to our lives. Every business or effort in which he was involved had to have a purpose because "purpose sustains you in good times and bad; if you've got a lock on purpose, it gives you energy and keeps you focused."

Five Principles drive an individual to develop a purpose mindset:

1. **Discovering Strengths**—focusing on strengths and building on them to create greater possibilities.
2. **Working from Abundance**—accessing a variety of innovative resources, from people to equipment and space, at previously unthinkable scales.
3. **Extending the Common Good**—moving from doing things efficiently to having an impact on broad community progress.
4. **Igniting Movements**—focusing on building a movement, not an organization, that leads to societal change.
5. **Embracing Empathy and Compassion**—centering on the "we" rather than the "me."

Discovering Strengths

We are accustomed to focusing on finding solutions to problems, to what's wrong. The idea of Appreciative Inquiry, a management principle developed by David Cooperrider and Suresh Srivastva at Case Western Reserve University, tries to refocus us on what works. At Cooperrider's workshop in 1994, I discovered their model of working from one's strengths: I learned our lives are not a problem to be solved but a mystery to be embraced.

Roberto D'Angelo and Francesca Fedeli abandoned their initial approach of trying to solve their son Mario's challenges and eventually embraced an approach of working with his strengths. Mario was a gift—they stopped fixating on the part of him that was not working and started focusing on what was working and how they could improve his strengths. Having purpose is about envisioning the world you want to be part of rather than fixing what's not working.

Working from Abundance

There will always be resources we have and resources we need. The challenge is whether we focus on what we have or on what we need. Balancing between what one has and what one needs is a constant struggle. The opportunity is to move into an abundance mode from a scarcity mode. Can we go from "there will never be enough" to "there is more than enough" if we harness resources more creatively? With new digital platforms, we can access a multitude of resources at previously unthinkable scales. Kevin Wang, Arpita and Rajeev Agarwal, and John Wood have all accessed this abundance.

Wang overcame a scarcity of qualified teachers to teach high school computer science by tapping into a network of computer science professionals willing to be trained and to volunteer as teachers, thereby scaling the program. Similarly, Wood created a distributed network of supporters who were willing to adopt a small library, which then enabled him to scale to more than thirty thousand schools. Arpita and Rajeev Agarwal also use the network effect to scale their efforts to reach half a million students in the Indian state of Uttar Pradesh.

Extending the Common Good

In our work and in our life, we constantly focus on ensuring that we are doing things well and efficiently. But efficiency may come at the expense of impacting broad community progress and the well-being of the planet. By focusing on broad community progress, we also amplify bridging networks, which extends our reach beyond personal and business growth to community well-being.

Claire Bonilla recognized she could harness her staff's strong skills in cornea recovery by motivating them to teach other doctors in India the same skills. Tony Mestres re-created the mission of the Seattle Foundation to embody working from both heart and science. He attracted new and younger supporters and has put the Seattle Foundation at the forefront of the COVID-19 response in Seattle. They have each brought a different mindset to their work, but eventually they understood that the work they were doing was very different from being in a corporation—the work was about extending the common good and not about gaining efficiency.

Igniting Movements

We have come to rely on the fact that organizations are powerful tools for achieving scale. But many efforts are now increasingly moving away from building organizations toward igniting movements. By using social media and online mobilization tools, one can weave together an activist network. Organizational skills are not what's needed but the skill and ability to inspire and synchronize movements. In the current COVID-19 environment, we see the emerging importance of these synchronizing skills. Through the use of platforms and other mobilizing tools, masses of people can synchronize efforts, such as the 100 Million Mask Challenge described previously, and can create social movements rather than just building and managing organizations. The Black Lives Matter movement is another effort where we are seeing distributed networks mobilizing around the world to address systematic racism and social injustice.

By working with the Global Give Back Circle, Margo Day has helped build a flexible network of women from multiple companies to provide mentorship to girls in Africa and India. In doing so, she has helped a small organization extend its impact. In a similar fashion, Hadi Partovi has created a movement around Code.org, mobilizing millions of teachers and students around the world to learn coding. Social Venture Partners has also been able to scale because, instead of creating a large, centrally managed global organization, it has created a flexible approach, which lets individual chapters synchronize their own efforts. Movements are not driven by leaders—they are driven by people who believe in an idea and continue to drive the movement forward.

Moving to Compassion and Kindness

In this time of crisis, we are witnessing increased acts of kindness: volunteers are stepping forward to help. Many people are beginning to realize that altruism and self-interest are not as far apart as they had thought. Will kindness become a more sustainable part of our societies when this crisis ends? Matthew Syed, the author of *Rebel Ideas: The Power of Diverse Thinking*, writes that people with a giving approach flourish in a world in which we are interdependent. He cites a study of six hundred medical students, which found that selfish students were more successful in the first year but students who were more generous—the "givers"—eventually thrived because of the transition from independent classes into clinical rotation and patient care.[27] As we move into a more interdependent society, people who are generous givers are more apt to succeed.

Kindness expands. It evolves from having a sense of *sympathy*, when we feel a moral obligation to lend a hand to someone in distress, to *empathy*, when we experience the plights or pains of others (especially those close to us), to *compassion*, when a deep sense of empathy is followed by the profound urge to alleviate the pain of strangers.

Most of us sit somewhere along this spectrum; this book highlights strategic givers who are on this path toward achieving compassion. As an African American woman in the tech sector, Trish Millines Dziko harnessed that sense of deep empathy in training minority students to excel in STEM. Andrea Taylor, on the other hand, brings her life's work, experience, and deep understanding of the community to full fruition at the Birmingham Civil Rights Institute. A purpose mindset puts us on that journey to becoming an empathetic and compassionate individual. By doing so, at scale we elevate our existence and promote flourishing, and cumulatively add to the common good.

Ideas Conquering the World

Changing the world through ideas is hard. British journalist Helen Lewis in her groundbreaking book *Difficult Women* describes the different roles that have to be played in any movement, often necessitating uneasy alliances and compromises, personal sacrifices, and at times the deliberate rocking of boats and taking of risks. We are seeing this in the Black Lives Matter movement where defunding the police is an important conversation that is challenging the status quo and creating uneasy allyship. A profound sense of purpose is an aspirational goal that keeps us together and keeps us moving towards a better world, towards a better ideal. This book highlights the principles that will help each of us start on that path. Though these principles are malleable and inexhaustible, my journey has been guided by my strengths, creating an environment of abundance, extending the common good, igniting movements, and discovering new ways to synchronize efforts rather than manage them. I keep moving toward developing compassion rather than being driven by passion, and in doing so I am continuously replenishing my energy source to care and do good.

Brad Smith, president of Microsoft, says that the company's employees connect to purpose in three different areas. The first is a sense of purpose in their day jobs. Smith stresses that this will always be the most important source of purpose for most employees since this is why they come to work in the morning and work is where they spend most of their time. The second is their opportunities to connect with other employees, particularly through activities like hackathons. The third is the giving program. This includes events associated with the October giving campaign, which have become fixtures of company culture. According to Smith, the purpose mindset and mission-driven orientation are central to everything Microsoft does, and it imbues itself in every corner of the company. He sees this as closely linked with the learn-it-all mindset that is also so important for Microsoft employees.

I think the time is now for us to shift the way we live and conduct business. Given the current COVID-19 environment, where the line between work and home has become even more blurred, providing opportunities for individuals to develop their purpose is more crucial than ever. This pandemic *may* send us down a path of new values.

Ultimately, every great purpose is a human purpose. This book offers examples of how businesses must foster a sense of purpose, particularly among their employees, if they want to survive and thrive. Businesses should become the main drivers behind an individual's sense of purpose: the survival of humanity depends on it.

ENDNOTES

INTRODUCTION

1. Erika Fry, Saving a City: "How Seattle's Corporate Giants Banded Together to Flatten the Curve," *Fortune*, April 17, 2020. Accessed at https://fortune .com/longform/coronavirus-seattle-flatten-curve-amazon-microsoft -starbucks-nordstrom-costco-covid-19-outbreak/.

2. "2019 Edelman Trust Barometer," Edelman.com, January 20, 2019. Accessed at https://www.edelman.com/research/2019-edelman-trust-barometer.

3. "Business Roundtable Redefines the Purpose of a Corporation to Promote 'An Economy That Serves All Americans,'" Business Roundtable, press release, August 19, 2019. Accessed at https://www.businessroundtable.org /business-roundtable-redefines-the-purpose-of-a-corporation-to-promote -an-economy-that-serves-all-americans.

4. Archie B. Carroll. "A History of Corporate Social Responsibility: Concepts and Practices," chapter 2 in *The Oxford Handbook of Corporate Social Responsibility* (Oxford University Press, 2008), pp.19–46. DOI 10.1093/oxfordhb /9780199211593.003.0002. https://www.researchgate.net/publication /282746355_A_History_of_Corporate_Social_Responsibility_Concepts_and _Practices.

5. Adam Weinger, "7 Outstanding Corporate Matching Gift Programs," America's Charities, November 3, 2016. Accessed at https://www.charities.org /news/blog/7-outstanding-corporate-matching-gift-programs.

6. Shobhit Seth, "World's Top 10 Software Companies," Investopedia, May 5, 2019. Accessed at https://www.investopedia.com/articles/personal-finance /121714/worlds-top-10-software-companies.asp.

7. "List of Public Corporations by Market Capitalization," Wikipedia. Accessed at https://en.wikipedia.org/wiki/List_of_public_corporations_by_market_ capitalization#2019.

8. "Ashesi University," Wikipedia. Accessed at https://en.wikipedia.org/wiki/Ashesi_University.

9. Aaron Hurst, *The Purpose Economy: How Your Desire for Impact, Personal Growth and Community Is Changing the World* (Imperative Press, 2018), p. 81.

10. David Brooks, *The Second Mountain: The Quest for a Moral Life* (Random House, 2019), p. xxii.

11. Caterina Bulgarella, "Five Ps Pave the Way to Purpose at Microsoft," *Forbes*, June 11, 2019. Accessed at https://www.forbes.com/sites/caterinabulgarella/2019/06/11/five-ps-pave-the-way-to-purpose-at-microsoft/#59e71b8379a2.

12. A selection of Dr. King's "Where Do We Go From Here" speech delivered August 16, 1967, to the Southern Christian Leadership Conference in Atlanta.

CHAPTER 1

1. Bill Gates Sr. with Mary Ann Macklin, *Showing Up for Life* (Broadway Books, 2009).

2. N. Craig Smith, "The New Corporate Philanthropy," *Harvard Business Review*, May–June 1994. Accessed at https://hbr.org/1994/05/the-new-corporate-philanthropy.

3. Sarah Ford, "Apple's Employee Matching Gift Program Yields More Than $50 Million for Charity," America's Charities, October 7, 2014. Accessed at https://www.charities.org/news/apples-employee-matching-gift-program-yields-more-50-million-charity.

4. Adam Weinger, "7 Outstanding Corporate Matching Gift Programs."

5. "U.N. Official praises Microsoft Employees for Helping Refugees," Microsoft, press release, July 6, 2000. Accessed at https://news.microsoft.com/2000/07/06/u-n-official-praises-microsoft-employees-for-helping-refugees/.

6. "Global Vision Impairment Facts," The International Agency for the Prevention of Blindness. Accessed at www.iapb.org/vision-2020/who-facts/.

7. "L V Prasad Eye Institute Launches Mobility & Sensory Stimulation Park, HelpLine for Visually Impaired," Microsoft India, press release, September 27, 2013. Accessed at https://news.microsoft.com/en-in/l-v-prasad-eye-institute-launches-mobility-sensory-stimulation-park-helpline-for-visually-impaired/.

8. "Microsoft, L V Prasad Eye Institute and Global Experts Collaborate to Launch Microsoft Intelligent Network for Eyecare," Microsoft India, press release, December 19, 2016. Accessed at https://news.microsoft.com/en-in/microsoft-l-v-prasad-eye-institute-and-global-experts-collaborate-to-launch-microsoft-intelligent-network-for-eyecare/.

9. Sidhartha, "Companies Law Set to Mandate 2% CSR Spend," *Times of India*, February 10, 2011. Accessed at https://timesofindia.indiatimes.com/india/Companies-law-set-to-mandate-2-CSR-spend/articleshow/7464529.cms.

10. "Corporate Responsibility," Microsoft. Accessed at https://www.microsoft .com/en-us/corporate-responsibility.

CHAPTER 2

1. Mark Sharfman, "Changing Institutional Roles: The Evolution of Corporate Philanthropy, 1883–1953," *Business & Society* 33, no. 3 (December 1994), pp. 236–269.
2. Michele Lent Hirsch, "America's Company Towns, Then and Now," *Smithsonian*, September 4, 2015. Accessed at https://www.smithsonianmag.com /travel/americas-company-towns-then-and-now-180956382/.
3. F. E. Andrews, *Corporations Giving* (Russell Sage Foundation, 1952), p. 24.
4. "Company Towns," *Slavery by Another Name*, PBS. Accessed at https://www.pbs .org/tpt/slavery-by-another-name/themes/company-towns/.
5. Helmuth von Moltke the Elder, "On Strategy" (1871), reprinted in *Militarische Werke* (1900).
6. David Dykstra, "The Mansions on Lake Washington Waterfront," Seattle Mansions, February 22, 2010. Accessed at http://seattle-mansions.blogspot .com/2010/02/nathan-myhrvolds-t-rex-house.html).
7. Intellectual Ventures homepage. Accessed at https://www.intellectual ventures.com/.
8. Institute for Disease Modeling InfoHub. Accessed at https://covid.idmod .org/#/).
9. Mifos X homepage. Accessed at https://mifos.org/.
10. "Responsible AI," Microsoft. Accessed at https://www.microsoft.com/en -us/ai/responsible-ai .
11. Philip Pullellia and Jeffrey Dastin, "Vatican Joins IBM, Microsoft to Call for Facial Recognition Regulation," Reuters, February 28, 2020. Accessed at https://www.reuters.com/article/us-vatican-artificial-intelligence-idUSKCN 20M0Z1 .
12. Jean-Philippe Courtois, "Creating a World of Good: Microsoft Launches the Global Scoail Entrepreneurship Program," Microsoft, February 21, 2020. Accessed at https://blogs.microsoft.com/blog/2020/02/21/creating-a -world-of-good-microsoft-launches-the-global-social-entrepreneurship -program/.
13. Live for Good homepage. Accessed at https://live-for-good.org/fr/.
14. Plast'if homepage. Accessed at https://plastif.com.
15. Clear Fashion homepage. Accessed at http://en.clear-fashion.com/.
16. Whire homepage. Accessed at https://www.whire.me/.

CHAPTER 3

1. Agnus Deaton, *The Great Escape: Health, Wealth, and the Origins of Inequality* (Princeton University Press, 2014). Accessed at https://press.princeton .edu/books/hardcover/9780691153544/the-great-escape.
2. Jim Yong Kim, "World Bank Group President Jim Yong Kim's Remarks at the International Forum on China's Reform and Opening Up and Poverty Reduction," The World Bank, November 1, 2018. Accessed at https://www .worldbank.org/en/news/speech/2018/11/01/world-bank-group -president-jim-yong-kim-remarks-at-the-international-forum-on-chinas -reform-and-opening-up-and-poverty-reduction.
3. Dylan Matthews, "23 Charts and Maps That Show the World Is Getting Much, Much Better," Vox, October 17, 2018. Accessed at https://www.vox.com /2014/11/24/7272929/global-poverty-health-crime-literacy-good-news.
4. "Inequality Crisis Worsens as World Bank and IMF Persist with Failed Policies," Bretton Woods Project, April 4, 2019. Accessed at https://www .brettonwoodsproject.org/2019/04/inequality-crisis-worsens-as-bank -and-imf-persist-with-failed-policies/.
5. Bob Young, "A Centennial Celebration of Suffrage: Trish Millines Dziko, 'You Have It; You Share It," *Seattle Times*, August 11, 2019. Accessed at https://www .seattletimes.com/pacific-nw-magazine/a-centennial-celebration-of-suffrage -trish-millines-dziko-you-have-it-you-share-it/.
6. Raj Kumar, *The Business of Changing the World: How Billionaires, Tech Disrupters, and Social Entrepreneurs Are Transforming the Global AID Industry* (Beacon Press, 2019).
7. Arne Duncan, "Education: The 'Great Equalizer,'" Encyclopedia Britannica. Accessed at https://www.britannica.com/topic/Education-The-Great -Equalizer-2119678#ref1255149.
8. Arne Duncan, "Education: The 'Great Equalizer.'"
9. Arne Duncan, "Education: The 'Great Equalizer.'"
10. Rajeev Agarwal, *What I Did Not Learn At IIT* (Penguin Books, India, 2013).
11. "Global Learning: XPRIZE Executive Summary," XPRIZE, August 22, 2019. Accessed at https://www.xprize.org/prizes/global-learning/articles/glexp -executive-summary .

CHAPTER 4

1. Robert Reich, *The Common Good* (Alfred A. Knopf, 2018), front inside flap.
2. "The Cleveland Foundation," Wikipedia. Accessed at https://en.wikipedia .org/wiki/The_Cleveland_Foundation.
3. Jimmy Carter, "TAP: The Power of a Project," October 17, 1995. Accessed at https://www.cartercenter.org/news/documents/doc58.html.
4. Seattle Children's Alliance homepage. Accessed at www.childrensallaince.org.

5. George McCully, *Philanthropy Reconsidered* (Catalogue for Philanthropy, 2008), p. 13.
6. Giuliana Gemelli, "Venture Philanthropy," in Helmut K. Anheier, Stefan Toeple (eds.), *International Encyclopedia of Civil Society* (Springer, 2010), p. 1606.
7. Jame Chen, "Impact Investing," Investopedia, October 9, 2019. Accessed at https://www.investopedia.com/terms/i/impact-investing.asp.
8. Abhilash Mudaliar, Rachel Bass, Hannah Dithrich, and Noshin Nova, "Annual Impact Investor Survey, 2019," Global Impact Investing Network, US-AID, June 2019. Accessed at https://thegiin.org/assets/GIIN_2019%20Annual%20Impact%20Investor%20Survey_webfile.pdf.
9. Unitus Ventures homepage. Accessed at https://unitus.vc/.
10. World Vision homepage. Accessed at www.worldvision.org.
11. Global Give Back Circle homepage. Accessed at https://www.globalgiveback circle.org/.

CHAPTER 5

1. David Brooks, *The Second Mountain: The Quest for a Moral Life* (Random House, 2019).
2. Kailash Satyarthi Children's Foundation homepage. Accessed at https://www.satyarthi.org.in/.
3. Social Venture Partners homepage. Accessed at http://www.socialventure partners.org/who-we-are/.
4. "Project Shiksha," Microsoft empowering educators. Accessed at https://www.microsoft.com/en-in/about/empowering-educators-shiksha.aspx.
5. Generation Unlimited homepage. Accessed at https://www.generation unlimited.org/.
6. "India Will Be Home to 10,500 Start-Ups by 2020: Report," *The Hindu*, October 26, 2016 (updated December 2, 2016). Accessed at https://www.thehindu.com/business/Industry/India-will-be-home-to-10500-start-ups-by-2020-Report/article16082376.ece.
7. "Global Entrepreneurship Index," The Global Enterprise and Development Institute, 2018 rankings. Accessed at https://thegedi.org/global-entrepreneurship-and-development-index/.
8. "Mastercard Index of Women Entrepreneurs, 2017," Mastercard newsroom. Accessed at https://newsroom.mastercard.com/wp-content/uploads/2017/03/Report-Mastercard-Index-of-Women-Entrepreneurs-2017-Mar-3.pdf.
9. Generation Unlimited homepage. Accessed at https://www.generation unlimited.org/.
10. "Sustainable Development Goals," United Nations. Accessed at https://www.un.org/sustainabledevelopment/sustainable-development-goals/.

11.	Aimee Groth, "Entrepreneurs don't have a special gene for risk—they come from families with money," Quartz, July 17, 2015. Accessed at https://qz.com/455109/entrepreneurs-dont-have-a-special-gene-for-risk-they-come-from-families-with-money/.

12.	Insight Assessment homepage. Accessed at https://www.insightassessment.com/.

13.	Akhtar Badshah, "The Blockchain Experiments Have Begun: Here's What They Could Yield for Business and Development," Next Billion, September 17, 2018. Accessed at https://nextbillion.net/blockchain-for-business-development.

14.	Tyler Schmall, "A Shocking Number of Americans Never Leave Home," New York Post, January 11, 2018. Accessed at https://nypost.com/2018/01/11/a-shocking-number-of-americans-never-leave-home/.

15.	"ILike," Wikipedia. Accessed at https://en.wikipedia.org/wiki/ILike.

16.	David Gelles, "Hadi Partovi Was Raised in a Revolution. Today He Teaches Kids to Code," New York Times, January 17, 2019. Accessed at https://www.nytimes.com/2019/01/17/business/hadi-partovi-code-org-corner-office.html.

17.	Code.org homepage. Accessed at https://code.org/.

CHAPTER 6

1.	Nicholas Kristof, "The Trader Who Donates Half His Pay," New York Times, April 4, 2015. Accessed at https://www.nytimes.com/2015/04/05/opinion/sunday/nicholas-kristof-the-trader-who-donates-half-his-pay.html?smid=nytcore-ios-share.

2.	Raj Kumar, The Business of Changing the World (Beacon Press, 2019), p. 140.

3.	Kim Malcolm and Andy Hurst, "You're Compassionate, So Why Aren't You Helping Homeless People? Shankar Vedantam Explains," KUOW, NPR, October 5, 2019. Accessed at https://www.kuow.org/stories/you-re-compassionate-so-why-aren-t-you-helping-homeless-people-shankar-vedantam-explains.

4.	"Leadership Case Study: Patrick Awuah," John P. McNulty Prize, McNulty Foundation, 2017. Accessed at mcnultyfound.org/files/McNulty-Case-Study_Patrick-Awuah.pdf.

5.	"Leadership Case Study: Patrick Awuah."

6.	"What You Can Do, or Dream You Can, Begin It; Boldness Has Genius, Power, and Magic in It," Quote Investigator, February 9, 2016. Accessed at https://quoteinvestigator.com/2016/02/09/boldness/.

7.	Mohammed Yunus, A World of Three Zeros: The New Economics of Zero Poverty, Zero Unemployment, and Zero Net Carbon Emissions (Public Affairs, 2017).

8.	"YY Ventures, Creating a World of Three Zeroes," Vimeo, May 20, 2020. Accessed at https://vimeo.com/420641332.

9. "History of Libraries," Wikipedia. Accessed at https://en.wikipedia.org /wiki/History_of_libraries .

10. Theodore Jones, *Carnegie Libraries across America* (Preservation Press, 1997).

11. Room to Read homepage. Accessed at https://www.roomtoread.org/impact -reach/.

12. Robert D'Angelo, "'Consider What You Have as a Gift and What You Lack as an Opportunity': What I Learned from My Son's Perinatal Stroke," Medium, July 27, 2017. Accessed at https://medium.com/microsoft-design /consider-what-you-have-as-a-gift-and-what-you-lack-as-an-opportunity -5ee9bac2ca87).

13. "Mirrorable Online," Fight the Stroke. Accessed at https://en.fightthestroke .org/mirrorablefaqpage.

14. "Microsoft Hackathon Champion Wins the Prize of Saving Lives," Dynamic Consultants Group. Accessed at https://www.dynamicconsultants group.com/blog/microsoft-hackathon-champion-wins-the-prize-of -saving-lives/.

CHAPTER 7

1. Tristan Claridge, "What Is the Difference between Bonding and Bridging Social Capital," Social Capital Research and Training, January 2, 2018. Accessed at https://www.socialcapitalresearch.com/difference-bonding -bridging-social-capital/.

2. "100 Million Mask Challenge," Providence.org. Accessed at https://www .providence.org/lp/100m-masks.

3. Michelle Toh, "JD.com Is Hiring 20,000 People Who Can't Work because of the Coronavirus," CNN Business, February 12, 2020. Accessed at https://amp .cnn.com/cnn/2020/02/12/tech/alibaba-jd-workers-china-coronavirus /index.html; Monica Nickelsburg and Todd Bishop, "Internal Memo: Jeff Bezos Tells Amazon Employees He's 'Wholly Focused' on the COVID-19 Crisis," GeekWire, March 21, 2020. Accessed at https://www.geekwire .com/2020/internal-memo-jeff-bezos-tells-amazon-employees-hes -wholly-focused-covid-19-crisis/.

4. Agnieszka de Sousa, Megan Durisin, and Manisha Jha, "Restaurant Suppliers Are Stuck with Tons of Unsold Food," Bloomberg, March 22, 2020. Accessed at https://www.bloomberg.com/news/articles/2020-03-22 /restaurant-suppliers-are-stuck-with-tons-of-unsold-food.

5. "Restaurant Owners Appreciate Landlord's Advice to 'Pay Employees' Instead of Rent," KAIT8 News, March 18, 2020. Accessed at https://www.kait8 .com/2020/03/18/property-owner-tells-restaurants-pay-employees -instead-rent/?fbclid=IwAR3YXye_5nmncI8TqG2ti8ofSVMYTy0L -y57OVJTO8fKIvhuoCC3NexjCoM.

6. COVID-19 Response Fund, Seattle Foundation. Accessed at https://www
.seattlefoundation.org/communityimpact/civic-leadership/covid-19
-response-fund.

7. All In Seattle homepage. Accessed at https://allinseattle.org/.

8. David Streitfeld, "A New Mission for Nonprofits During the Outbreak:
Survival," *New York Times*, March 27, 2020. Accessed at https://www
.nytimes.com/2020/03/27/business/nonprofits-survival-coronavirus
.html?referringSource=articleShare.

9. "Responding to COVID-19 Together," Microsoft. Accessed at https://news
.microsoft.com/covid-19-response/.

10. "UNICEF and Microsoft Launch Global Learning Platform to Help Address
COVID-19 Education Crisis," Microsoft, press release, April 19, 2020. Accessed at https://news.microsoft.com/2020/04/19/unicef-and-microsoft
-launch-global-learning-platform-to-help-address-covid-19-education-crisis/.

11. "Microsoft launches initiative to help 25 million people worldwide acquire
the digital skills needed in a COVID-19 economy," Microsoft. Accessed at
https://blogs.microsoft.com/blog/2020/06/30/microsoft-launches
-initiative-to-help-25-million-people-worldwide-acquire-the-digital-skills
-needed-in-a-covid-19-economy/.

12. Anne Loehr, "How to Live with Purpose, Identify Your Values, and Improve
Your Leadership," Huffpost, December 6, 2017. Accessed at https://www
.huffpost.com/entry/how-to-live-with-purpose-_b_5187572.

13. Claudine Gartenberg and George Serafeim, "181 Top CEOs Have Realized
Companies Need a Purpose Beyond Profit," *Harvard Business Review*, August
20, 2019. Accessed at https://hbr.org/2019/08/181-top-ceos-have-realized
-companies-need-a-purpose-beyond-profit .

14. "Business Roundtable Redefines the Purpose of a Corporation to Promote
'An Economy That Serves All Americans,'" Business Roundtable, press release, August 19, 2019. Accessed at https://www.businessroundtable.org
/business-roundtable-redefines-the-purpose-of-a-corporation-to-promote
-an-economy-that-serves-all-americans.

15. "The B2B Purpose Paradox 2020: How Purpose Powers Business-to-Business
Growth," The Harris Poll, the ANA, and Carol Cone ON PURPOSE, July
2019. Accessed at https://d98b5d6b-d295-4c53-b7a5-033c419c6968.usrfiles
.com/ugd/d98b5d_e602c585f0184fed979e199c9049801a.pdf .

16. Hubert Joly, "A Time to Lead with Purpose and Humanity," *Harvard Business
Review*, March 24, 2020. Accessed at https://hbr.org/2020/03/a-time-to
-lead-with-purpose-and-humanity.

17. Geoff Baker, "Microsoft Push Brings Medical Supplies from Overseas to Aid
in State's Coronavirus Fight," *Seattle Times*, March 24, 2020. Accessed at
https://www.seattletimes.com/business/local-business/microsoft-push
-brings-medical-supplies-from-overseas-to-aid-in-states-coronavirus-fight/.

18. "Rockport Walk Test," Top End Sports. Accessed at https://www.topendsports
.com/testing/tests/rockport.htm.

19. Carol Cone ON PURPOSE, *Purpose 360*, Apple Podcasts. Accessed at https://podcasts.apple.com/us/podcast/purpose-360/id1442089764.

20. "Why Do Millennials Choose to Engage in Cause Movements?" The Millennial Impact Report, 2017. Accessed at http://www.themillennialimpact .com/.

21. "Why Do Millennials Choose to Engage in Cause Movements?" The Millennial Impact Report, 2017.

22. Satya Nadella, "Achieving More for the World," LinkedIn, January 19, 2020. Accessed at https://www.linkedin.com/pulse/achieving-more-world-satya -nadella/).

23. Mariana Mazzucato, *The Value of Everything: Making and Taking in the Global Economy* (Public Affairs, 2018), p. 5.

24. Jeff Corbin, "Surprising Results from the 2017 Gallup Employee Engagement Report," The Employee App, March 7, 2017. Accessed at https://www .theemployeeapp.com/gallup-2017-employee-engagement-report-results -nothing-changed/).

25. Robert Dur and Max van Lent, "Socially Useless Jobs," Tinbergen Institute Discussion Paper 18-034/VII, March 30, 2018. Accessed at https://papers .ssrn.com/sol3/papers.cfm?abstract_id=3162569.

26. Dominic Rushe, "Covid-19 a 'Wake-up Call' to Build Fairer Society, Says Billionaire JP Morgan Boss," *The Guardian*, May 19, 2020. Accessed at https://www.theguardian.com/business/2020/may/19/jamie-dimon -coronavirus-fairer-society-jp-morgan-ceo.

27. New Impact homepage. Accessed at https://www.newimpact.care/.

28. Matthew Syed, "Coronavirus: The Good That Can Come Out of an Upside Down World," BBC News, March 30, 2020. Accessed at https://www.bbc .com/news/world-us-canada-52094332.

INDEX

ABOUT THE AUTHOR

AKHTAR BADSHAH is a seasoned executive with more than thirty years of experience in international development, managing a corporate philanthropic program, and cofounding a global nonprofit for social enterprise. Dr. Badshah is Founder and Chief Catalyst at Catalytic Innovators Group, which advises individuals and organizations to catalyze their social and philanthropic investments. He is a Distinguished Practitioner at the University of Washington's Evans School of Public Policy and Governance and at the Business School, Bothell campus.

Dr. Badshah is also the founder and curator of Accelerating Social Transformation, a midcareer professional development certificate course on social impact. He led Microsoft's philanthropic efforts for ten years, where he administered the company's community investment and employee contributions. He was also instrumental in launching both Unlimited Potential and Youth Spark—the company's focus on bringing digital technology to the underserved communities and youth all over the world.

About the Microsoft Alumni Network Series

THE MICROSOFT ALUMNI NETWORK is a worldwide community of former employees who share a common experience of having worked at Microsoft. Founded in 1995, the Alumni Network is a member organization representing more than fifty thousand alumni in fifty-one countries. The Alumni Network publishing partnership with HarperCollins Leadership represents the broad range of talent that makes up the Microsoft alumni community: entrepreneurs, tech innovators, business professionals, nonprofit leaders, volunteers, and lifelong learners, while shining a light on the meaningful impact that Microsoft's alumni have around the globe.

LISTING OF SERIES BOOKS:

Back to Business: Finding Your Confidence, Embracing Your Skills, and Landing Your Dream Job after a Career Pause
Nancy McSharry Jensen and Sarah Duenwald

Purpose Mindset: How Microsoft Inspires Employees and Alumni to Change the World
Akhtar Badshah

Taking Charge of Change: How Real People Solve Hard Problems
Paul Shoemaker